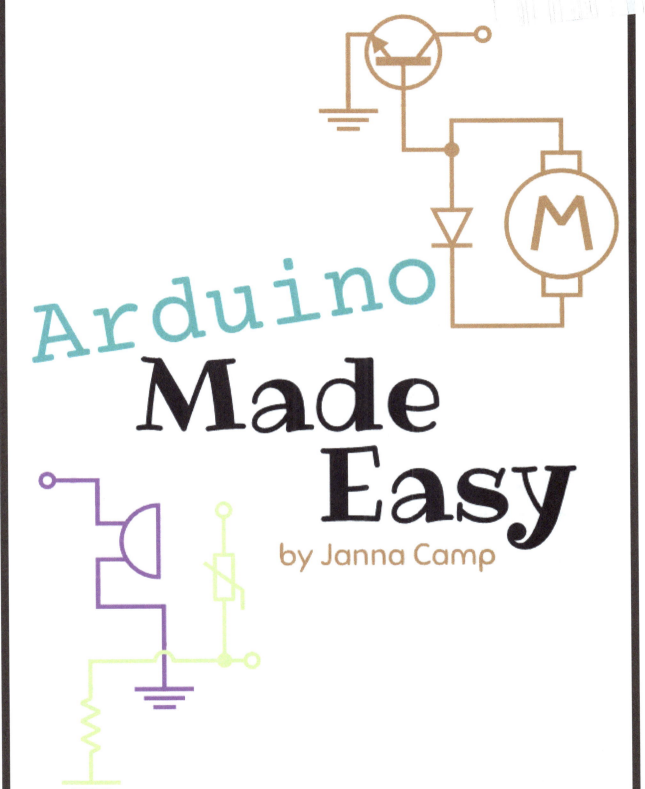

Arduino

Made Easy

by Janna Camp

KDP Hardcover ISBN: 9798329489880
KDP Paperback ISBN: 9798329489781

Credits:

Breadboard circuit pictures made using Fritzing.

Resistor Color Code Image:
Adim kassn, CC BY-SA 3.0 <https://creativecommons.org/licenses/by-sa/3.0>, via Wikimedia Commons

How an ultrasonic sensor works picture modified from:
Xabi22, CC BY-SA 4.0 <https://creativecommons.org/licenses/by-sa/4.0>, via Wikimedia Commons

DC Motor Simulation Picture:
Haade, CC BY-SA 3.0 <https://creativecommons.org/licenses/by-sa/3.0>, via Wikimedia Commons

Table of Contents

Introduction

Welcome to Arduino Made Easy!

I originally wrote this material when I was teaching a class of middle and high schoolers – many of whom were brand new to programming. (Though the content is relevant for those young and old alike!) I wanted the lessons to have a casual feel that would explain concepts in simple language. My goal was to teach the basics of programming and circuits, breaking things down into pieces that were easy to manage and giving learners the tools to use the concepts in their own projects. This book is designed to guide you through working with each component individually to give you the tools to be able to easily take the components and use them in designing them into your own projects. I hope that you find this book to be a helpful, fun experience to work through as you learn about the world of electronics.

–Janna Camp

Interested in teaching this in a class?

The material in this book is available as a complete course on Teachers Pay Teachers.

https://www.teacherspayteachers.com/store/janna-camp

Included files consist of PowerPoint slides, student reference sheets for each lesson, complete code files, and course reference documents as well as detailed supply and project lists. Plus, a digital copy of this book!

Parts List

Below is a list of all the supplies that will be used in this book. These can all be purchased individually, but that can get a bit expensive for a single person. There are a few Uno starter kits available (ELEGOO on Amazon or directly from Arduino) that contain most of what is needed – a checklist of parts for a couple of these kits is listed below.

Parts	Quantity Needed	ELEGOO UNO Project Super Starter Kit	ELEGOO UNO R3 Project Most Complete Starter Kit	Arduino Starter Kit
Uno Board	1	x	x	x
Male to Male Jumper Wires	---	x	x	x
Male to Female Jumper Wires	---	x	x	
Breadboard	1–2	x	x	x
220 ohm Resistors	12	x	x	x
10k ohm Resistors	8	x	x	x
Input Components				
Push Buttons (2-pin or 4-pin)	8	**	**	x
SPDT Slide Switch	1			
Tilt Switch	1	x	x	x
Potentiometers	3	**	**	x
Photoresistor	1		x	x
HC-SR04 Ultrasonic Sensor	1	x	x	
TMP36 Temperature Sensor	1			x
4x4 Membrane Keypad	1		x	
Output Components				
LEDs (Red, Yellow, Green)	12 (4 of each color)	x	x	x
RGB LED (Common Cathode)	1		x	x
Seven-segment display (1 Digit, Common Cathode)	1	x	x	
Piezo Buzzer	1	x	x	x
I2C 1602 LCD (16x2)	1			
Motor Components				
DC Motor	1	x	x	x
Diode (1N4001 or Similar)	1	x	x	x

Transistor (IRF520N MOSFET or Similar NPN)	1	x	x	x
9V Battery	1	x	x	
9V Battery Clip	1	x	x	x
SG90 Micro Servo	1	x	x	x
Stepper Motor 28BYJ–48 + ULN2003 Driver	1	x	x	

** These components come in this kit, but in a smaller quantity than needed.

Lesson 1 - Circuit Basics
Introduction to Electric Circuits

Introduction - What are electric circuits?

Electricity is the flow of electrons through materials. Electrons always flow from negative to positive (though flow in circuits is generally measured the other way – positive to negative, called current). We can utilize this flow in circuits we build to perform useful tasks by using various special components.

There are three important electrical terms that will help define measurements of many of the components that will be used – voltage, current, and resistance. Voltage is the "push" that moves charges through a wire or electrical component. It is measured in Volts. Current is the flow of electrons in a circuit. It is measured in Amps. Resistance is the opposition to current flow in a circuit. It is measured in Ohms.

An electric circuit is a combination of electric components arranged in a "loop." This includes a device that supplies voltage, components that use the current "pushed" by the voltage supply, and wires in which the current flows between components. Voltage will be addressed from the power source in terms of positive and negative (negative is often called ground). Current flows from the positive side of the voltage source to the negative side through the circuit.

Circuit Components - What makes up a circuit?

Breadboards

Breadboards are devices that allow us to build temporary circuits – circuits that don't require soldering. They have holes that arranged in rows and columns to connect circuit components. The two middle sections are connected in rows of 5. The outside sections are connected in columns.

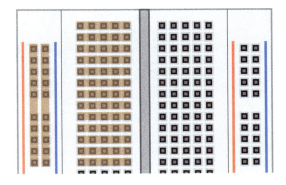

Resistors

Resistors are electrical components that resist the flow of electrons in a circuit – think of how a filter might resist the flow of water in a pipe. Common uses of resistors are to limit the current in a circuit, divide voltages, or adjust signal levels. The lessons in this book will primarily be using resistors to limit currents. Resistors have colored stripes that tell us what their value is.

Resistor Color Code:

The resistor color code is the code for determining the values of resistors. There are either 2 or 3 values (depending on if resistor is 4-band or 5-band) followed by a multiplier and tolerance. The tolerance, which is usually either 1% or 5%, is the percentage the actual resistor value might vary from the stated value.

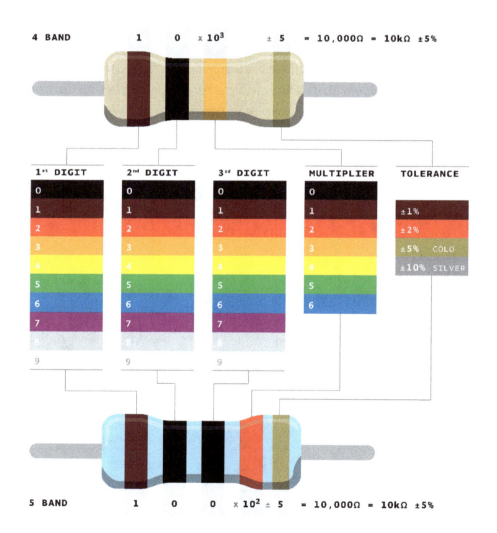

8

Light Emitting Diodes (LEDs)

Diodes are electrical components that allow current to flow only one direction. This can be helpful in preventing current from flowing the wrong way (we will discuss this more later). LEDs are a special form of diode that produce light when current goes through them. They can be used any place a light is needed – for example as illumination or an indicator. The long leg of an LED goes on the positive side of the circuit.

Push Buttons

Push buttons are simple switches that are used in electric circuits. A button is attached to two parts of a circuit but will only connect them together when it is pushed down. You may also sometimes see them called momentary switches. Often, push buttons have four leads (wires to connect to breadboard) which are connected in pairs, but to make the circuits easier, the ones in this book have two leads.

Toggle Switches (SPDT)

Toggle switches are another type of simple switch that we can use in electric circuits. SPDT stands for "single pole double throw." These types of toggle switches have three legs. Whichever direction the switch is toggled to, the end pin on that side will connect to the middle pin. While there are other types of toggle switches, this is the only type this book will be using.

Power Supplies

A power supply is any component that provides voltage and current to a circuit. For our purposes, this could be a battery, a device that plugs into a wall, or an Arduino board.

Circuit Diagrams

In this book, we will be using two types of circuit diagrams – breadboard diagrams and circuit schematics. While both will be used for each circuit given throughout this book, circuit schematics are the more common diagram so it is important that you learn how to read and understand them.

Breadboard Diagrams

Breadboard diagrams are pictures that show an example breadboard view of a circuit. Components will be placed just as they might be on a physical breadboard. Wires connect components as needed. Anything connected directly to power or ground will be connected (either directly or using wires) to the corresponding rails/columns on the outside of the breadboard. The red rails will be used for power and the blue rails will be used for ground.

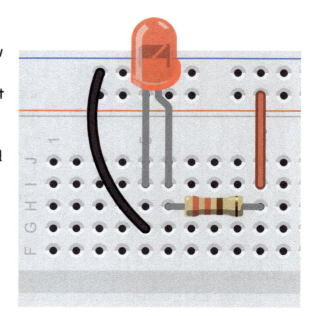

Generally red wires will connect to power, black wires will connect to ground, and other colors will be used for any other connection. While wire color does not matter when it comes to functionality of your circuit, it is worth keeping in mind to help to keep your circuit organized.

Circuit Schematics

Circuit schematics are diagrams that show exactly what components are needed in a circuit and where to connect them. However, they are organized for clarity, not for the actual locations in which the circuit is built on a breadboard. Each component is represented by a specific symbol, and

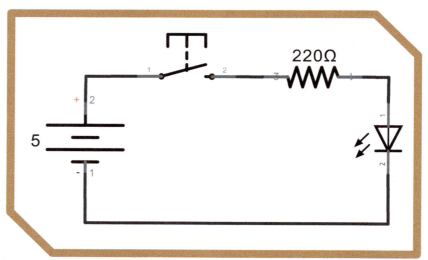

often with a value or some other marking to label each individual part. Circuit schematics will be shown in orange boxes throughout this book.

Circuit Symbols

As new components are added throughout this book, new symbols will be added as well. The symbols that are used will be consistent through all the schematics in this book but may vary slightly to what you find elsewhere. This is because while some symbols are very standard, others are a bit more specialized and can vary from place to place (different authors, schematic programs, etc.). Circuit symbols will be shown in teal boxes with labels. Here are the first few circuit symbols that will be used:

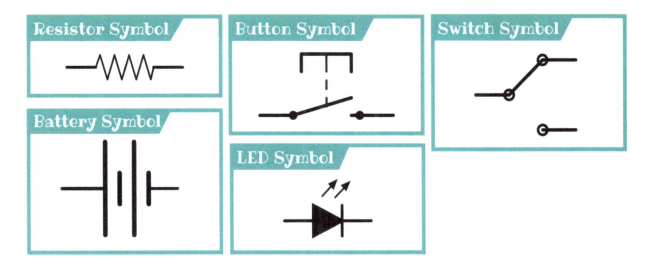

Activity - Let's Build Some Circuits!

You will be building LED circuits in this activity. Each circuit will contain a DC power source (5V), a resistor (to limit the current – the value of a current-limiting resistor is calculated based on the specifications of the LED and the voltage of the power source), and an LED.

Circuit 1 - LED circuit

The first circuit you will build contains a single LED and current-limiting resistor (220 ohms). The resistor could go on either side of the resistor, as long as it is in the circuit it

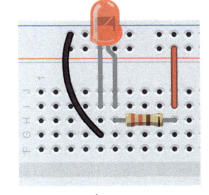

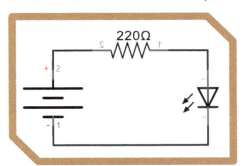

will do its job of limiting the current. In this case, it has been placed from the positive power rail to the positive lead of the LED. The negative side of the LED connects the negative/ground rail. The power/ground rails can connect directly to your power source. This is listed as 5 V in the schematic and if you use your Arduino as your power source that will be the case. A 9V battery also works well as a power source for this circuit.

Circuit 2 - LED Button Circuit

For the second circuit, you will be adding a button into your circuit. With it, the light will only turn on when the button is pressed. Pull

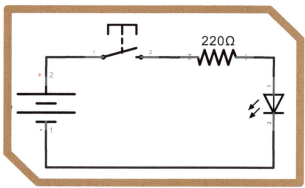

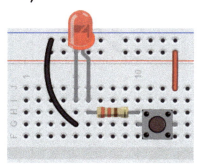

your circuit apart in one spot and insert the button. This can be anywhere, though the diagrams have it between the positive power connection and resistor.

Circuit 3 - Switch Circuit

For the third circuit, swap the button for a switch. The switch should connect using either

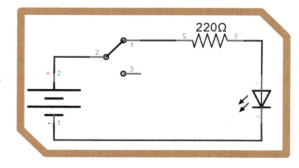

one of the outside pins and the center pin.

Bonus Circuit

As a bonus challenge, try adding a second LED and resistor the other side of the switch. With this setup, one light will be on when the switch is switched one direction, and the other light will be on when the switch is switched the other direction. The circuit diagrams for this circuit are in the solutions section at the back of the book.

Conclusion

In this lesson, you looked at some simple LED/button/switch circuits. In the next lesson, you will begin learning programming on the Arduino while using circuit principles learned in this lesson to create programmed circuits.

Lesson 2 - Welcome to Arduino
Introduction to Arduino

Introduction - What is an Arduino anyway?

Microcontrollers

A microcontroller is a special kind of circuit that works like a tiny computer. Microcontrollers use electrical signals to send data back and forth between themselves and various electrical components. They take input signals from components like buttons and sensors and then respond by sending output signals to components like lights, screens, and motors.

Arduino

Arduino is an Italian company that designs microcontroller boards and associated software programs. When Arduino was started in 2005, its founders had the goal of making it low-cost and easy for students and hobbyists to prototype and build microcontroller projects. Below are some examples of different Arduino boards:

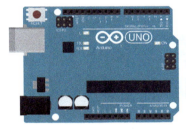
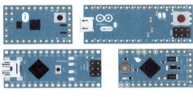
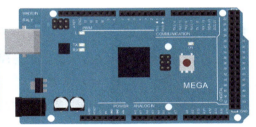

Get to Know Your Board - A little about your Arduino...

Uno

The Arduino Uno board will be used throughout this book. On the following page, the various parts of the board are outlined.

On the left side of the board, there is a USB port and power jack (Fig. 2a). The USB port is how the board is attached to the computer to program. The power jack can be used to power the board once it has been programmed.

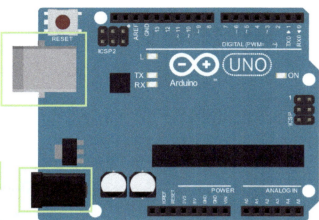

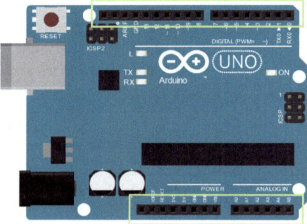

Figure 2a – USB Port and Power Jack

The pins that components will connect to are located along the top and bottom of the board (Fig. 2b). They have what are called headers that allow us to connect wires directly to them.

Figure 2b – Headers

Power Pins

The 3V3 pin outputs 3.3 volts. The 5V pin outputs 5 volts. The GND pins (two on the left, one on the right) are the ground pins – a bit like the negative side of the circuit. (Fig. 2c) Ground provides an electrical reference point for your components. The VIN pin is another option for providing power to your Arduino.

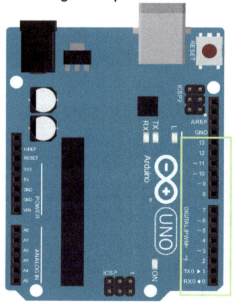

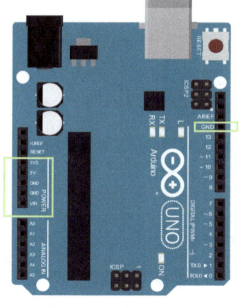

Figure 2c – Power Pins

Digital Pins

Digital pins (Fig. 2d) allow voltage to be represented in a single bit – either 0 (Low) or 1 (High) for off or on, respectively. Pins 0–13 are digital pins that are used for digital input or output. Pins 0–1 are normally used by the board for

Figure 2d – Digital Pins

something called the serial monitor so these won't typically be used for physical components. Pin 13 controls the on-board LED but can also be used for input or output to the pin for external components.

Analog Pins

Analog pins allow a variable voltage to be inputted. This would usually be something like a series of values

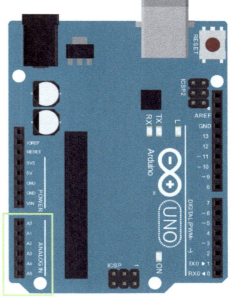

from a sensor. They convert the voltages to digital values that we can use to control digital output. There are 6 pins (A0–A5) that allow

Figure 2e – Analog Pins

analog input. All of the analog pins can also be used for digital input and output.

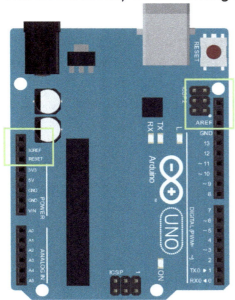

Figure 2f – Other Pins

Other Pins

There are a few other pins which are used for special kinds of communication with other devices. Some of these will be covered later.

Arduino Circuit Schematic

This is the schematic diagram for the Arduino Uno board. It consists of a box with pins for each of the pins on the board. It will also be labeled with the name of the board. As new components are added, a few will be in this style – a labeled box with pins.

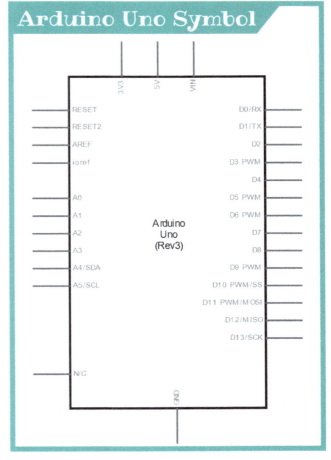

Programming Basics - Learn a Little Coding

Functions

Functions are small "modules" of code that work independently from one another. They allow you to write small sections of code that can be used by other code. They have a general form that looks like the following:

```
type functionName(type argument){

}
```

The type is the type of variable a function returns – for now the functions you use won't return a variable so their type will be void. functionName is the name of the function. For now, the functions used will be pre-defined so they will already be named. Function names follow the same rules as variable names which will be discussed in a bit. The function name is followed by a set of parentheses – ( ). These can contain variables that get passed to the function, called arguments. The function can use arguments to perform operations, set parameters, or do other tasks. Arguments must also be defined by a type. Multiple arguments can be separated by commas. Following the parentheses is a set of curly braces – { }. These will contain the code of the function. Most of the code you write will be inside various functions.

Writing a Program

When you open a new Arduino program (called a sketch), you will see two functions. The first one, setup will be where you write code that will run once, right when your program starts. The second one, loop will run after setup and will keep running as long as the Arduino has power connected.

```
void setup() {
  // put your setup code here, to run once:

}

void loop() {
  // put your main code here, to run repeatedly:

}
```

Little Gray Slashes (Comments)

As you may have noticed, in the previous Arduino

```
// put your setup code here, to run once:
// put your main code here, to run repeatedly:
```

program example, there are a couple lines that begin with two forward slashes. These lines are called comments. They are not actual code but are written in programs to give information to someone reading the code. Your computer will ignore them when running your code. Comments can be on a line by themselves or at the end of a line of code.

Using Functions

In addition to writing your own functions, there are lots of pre-written functions for you to use. To use them, you just write the name of the function along with a set of parentheses and pass any arguments that it needs (in the parentheses). As an example, suppose a function "addition" needs two integer arguments – let's use values 100 and 25. It would be said that you would "call" it like this: `addition(100, 25)`

PinMode Function

The first built-in function used will be the pinMode function. This will be used inside the setup function that will begin your programs when using digital pins. This function defines whether the digital pins you are using should be used for INPUT (getting information from a component) or OUTPUT (sending a signal to a component). The usage in code would look like this:

```
pinMode(pinNum, OUTPUT);
```

pinNum is the number of the digital pin (labeled on the board). It can be a variable that is assigned an integer value prior to calling the function, or you can just use an integer value in your function call.

DigitalWrite Function

The digitalWrite function sends a low (0V) or high value (5V) to the specified pin. This is useful for turning things on or off like LEDs. digitalWrite uses two arguments: a pin number and LOW/HIGH (which represent values 0 and 1). Usage would look like this:

```
digitalWrite(pinNum, HIGH);
```

To use the digitalWrite function, you must have your pin initialized to OUTPUT.

DigitalRead Function

The digitalRead function reads a value (high or low) from a specified pin. This is useful in detecting button pushes or switch positions. digitalRead uses one argument: a pin number. Usage would look like this:

```
digitalRead(pinNum);
```

To use the digitalRead function, you must have your pin initialized to INPUT.

Delay Function

The delay function accepts one argument – an integer value, which represents a time in milliseconds. When the program encounters this function, it waits the specified number of milliseconds before moving on to the next line of code. This line of code delays the program by 1000 milliseconds (1 second):

```
delay(1000);
```

Semicolons

You may have noticed that the function examples given have a semicolon at the end of each of them. A semicolon is how your compiler knows where the end of each line of code is (also called a statement). Therefore, at the end of each line you write, you will need to write a semicolon. In fact, semicolons are really only dividing statements, so technically, the statements don't even have to be on separate lines. It is good practice to use separate lines for readability, however. If you forget one, you will get something similar to the following error:

```
Compilation error: expected ';' before '}' token
```

Variables

Variables are named values that are stored in the processor's memory. They are defined or "declared" by naming their type, naming them, and then (optionally) setting them equal to a value. Here are some examples:

```
int myVariable = 10;
```

```
int myVariable;
```

Variables might retain the same value throughout the entirety of the program, or the program might change the value from time to time. To give a variable a new value, you write the name and set it equal to a new value:

```
myVariable = 7;
```

There are a few rules and conventions when naming variables (the same rules apply to function names as well). You almost always want to name your variables something useful – something that describes what your variable is for (there are a few exceptions to this which will come up later). Variable names can begin with a letter or underscore (_). Variable names can contain letters, numbers, or underscores. There are also several keywords in Arduino that cannot be used as variable names. These are words that are already defined within the Arduino language. Below is a list of the Arduino keywords:

abs	detachInterrupts	new	PD7	Serial
acos	digitalRead	null	PI	serialAvailable
analogRead	digitalWrite	OUTPUT	PINB	serialRead
analogWrite	DISPLAY	PB0	PINC	serialWrite
asin	do	PB1	PIND	Setup
atan	double	PB2	pinMode	shiftOut

atan2	else	PB3	PORTB	short
attachInterrupts	exp	PB4	PORTC	signed
available	FALLING	PB5	PORTD	sin
begin	float	PB6	print	sq
beginSerial	floor	PB7	printBinary	sqrt
boolean	for	PC0	printByte	static
byte	HALF_PI	PC1	printHex	switch
case	HIGH	PC2	printInteger	tan
ceil	if	PC3	println	this
CHANGE	INPUT	PC4	printNewline	throw
char	int	PC5	printOctal	try
class	log	PC6	printString	TWO_PI
constrain	long	PC7	private	unsigned
cos	loop	PD0	protected	void
DDRB	LOW	PD1	public	while
DDRC	LSBFIRST	PD2	pulseIn	write
DDRD	max	PD3	read	FALSE
default	millis	PD4	return	TRUE
delay	min	PD5	RISING	
delayMicroseconds	MSBFIRST	PD6	SERIAL	

Capital and lowercase letters are distinct/different in variable names. A variable named `MyVariable` will be different than a variable named `myvariable`. In most cases, this book will use the camel case naming convention when variable names have more than one word. The first word is lowercase and subsequent words begin with an uppercase letter. Something like: `thisIsMyVariableName`

Types of Variables
As previously stated, variables must be defined with a type. Some common types that may be used are:
- int – integer values (no decimals)
- float – floating point values (contain decimals)
- string – strings of characters including letters, numbers, and symbols (these will be written in quotation marks)
- bool – Boolean values (true or false – can also use 0 and 1)

Damage Control - Taking Care of Problems

Compiling

After writing your code, you will be ready to test it on your Arduino. Your Arduino, however doesn't understand the code as you wrote it. The code needs to go through a process called compilation – using something called a compiler. This is built into your IDE and will be done automatically but it is helpful to know that it is happening. The compiler takes your code and converts it into a language the Arduino can understand, called assembly language. Here is a short example of what assembly might look like:

```
ORR R12, R1, R2
JMP R16, 2
MOV R10, 48
SUB R0, R1, R2
```

Debugging - Dealing with Errors

It is possible (and likely!) that at times your compiler will fail. Things that cause your compiler to fail are called errors and it is necessary that you learn to interpret them and know how to fix them. Most of the time, the compiler will tell you exactly what the issue in your code is, so it will just take some practice in learning to read and interpret. The process of working through errors is called debugging.

Errors are problems in your code that prevent it from running either correctly or at all. There are three main types of errors that you will likely encounter – syntax, logic, and compilation.

Syntax errors are typos, much like grammar mistakes in your code, and are typically the easiest to fix. This could be incorrect or missed punctuation, misuse of operators, etc.

Compilation errors are any kind of error that causes the program to be unable to compile. This would include syntax errors but could also be things like misspelled words, wrong names, wrong types, etc. For these types of errors, your IDE will tell you what the problem is when they occur.

Logic errors will not necessarily cause your program to completely not run but may cause your program to run incorrectly, hence there is an error in your logic. This could be something like loops being written wrong or lines of code out of order.

Programming the Arduino - Introduction to the Arduino IDE

What is an IDE?

An IDE is an Integrated Development Environment. This is a program that allows you to edit, compile, and upload/run your code all from within a single window. Arduino has its own IDE that can be used to program Arduino boards. Here is a screenshot of what the Arduino IDE looks like:

In the next section, the different parts of the IDE will be explained.

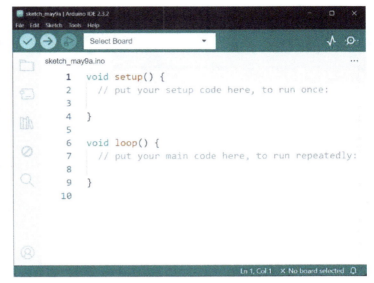

Getting around the IDE

This button uploads your code to the board (will compile too if that has not been done yet).

This box is where you will set up your board connection.

This button compiles your code.

These side panel buttons have some useful features that will be explored later.

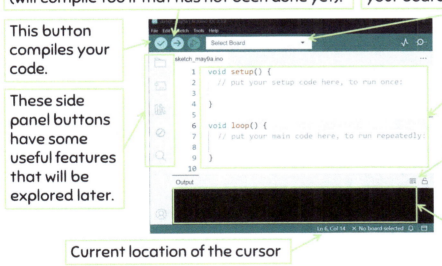

This is the area in which you will write your code.

Clears the output window.

This is where program output will show up (compilation success or errors).

Current location of the cursor

Activity - Blinky Blinky - Writing your First Program

In the program for this lesson, you will use the Arduino to blink an LED. Your goal will be to connect a digital pin of the Arduino to an LED and turn it on and off at regular intervals.

Schematics

Here is the schematic for the circuit you need to build. This circuit contains an LED and 220 ohm resistor. The resistor will prevent the circuit from drawing too much current which could damage your board. The value or "size" of this resistor is based on the input current and the specifications of the LED being used.

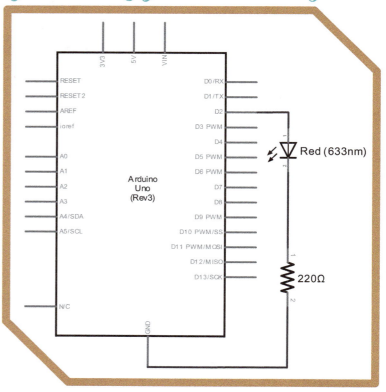

Here is the breadboard view of the circuit. Connect the positive side of the LED to digital pin 2, and the negative side of the LED to the resistor. The other side of the resistor will connect to ground. Remember, the middle sections of the breadboard are connected in rows of 5.

Program Outline and Code

Here is a general outline for your program. Remember, a new Arduino sketch opens containing two functions, setup and loop.

What does the setup function need?

You need to set up your pin. The LED is connected to pin 2. This will need to be an output signal so the board can send signals to the LED.

What does the loop function need?

In the main part of the program, you will blink the LED by turning it on, waiting a second, turning it off, and waiting another second. This loop will keep repeating so you only need to turn on and off once.

To write the program, begin by opening a new Arduino sketch. Here is the code for this activity:

```
void setup() {
  // put your setup code here, to run once:
  pinMode(2,OUTPUT);
}

void loop() {
  // put your main code here, to run repeatedly:
  digitalWrite(2,HIGH); //Turn LED on
  delay(1000); //Wait 1 second
  digitalWrite(2,LOW); //Turn LED off
  delay(1000); //Wait 1 second
}
```

Bonus Activity

The Arduino has a built-in LED that is connected to pin 13. Try replacing pin 2 in the program with 13 or LED_BUILTIN and see what happens.

Conclusion

Here is a quick overview of the topics covered in this lesson:

- What is a microcontroller/Arduino?
- Programming basics – functions, comments, and variables
- Finding and fixing errors
- Uploading a program to the Arduino

Through this lesson you should have a basic understanding of how to write a simple program, upload it to the Arduino, and successfully have a working circuit. In the next lesson, you will be working on developing and practicing coding logic skills. You will use concepts learned in this lesson to write your own programs.

Lesson 3 - Traffic Signals
Designing your first programs

Topic Review

- For this lesson's assignments, you don't need to learn any new concepts. Rather, you will be reviewing some of the things you learned in the last lesson, including:

    - Variables
    - Built-in functions – pinMode, delay, digitalWrite
    - LED circuits

Activity 1 - One-Way Traffic Signal

Overview

For the first assignment, you will be building a basic traffic signal with 3 LEDs – red, yellow, green. Your goal will be to turn on one LED at a time to simulate the normal cycling of a traffic signal. The timing on the lights will be the following:

- Red – 5 seconds
- Green – 5 seconds
- Yellow – 2 seconds

This pattern will continue looping indefinitely.

Schematic

The schematic for this circuit is pretty simple. You will use three LED/resistor circuits connected to three digital pins (2, 3, and 4).

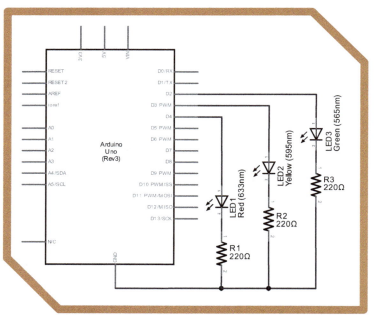

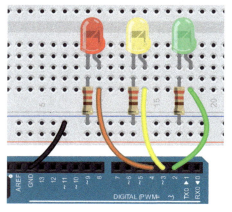

Breadboard Diagram

Here is the breadboard diagram. Red, yellow, and green LEDs are connected to pins 2, 3, and 4 on the positive side, and to 220 ohm resistors and ground on the negative sides.

Code Overview

Let's discuss what the code for this program needs.

What does the setup function need?

- pinMode functions for each pin to initialize to output
- Initial light values – start with the red light

What does the loop function need?

- delay function – 5 sec for red light
- change light values – red to green
- delay function – 5 sec for green light
- change light values – green to yellow
- delay function – 2 sec for yellow light
- change light values – yellow to red – Since the red light was where we started, the delay function at the beginning of the loop will be the delay needed for the red light.

Code

Before the setup function you will use some integer variables to hold the pin values. This makes it easier to remember which pin is which. By placing the variables outside the setup function, it allows them to be accessed by both the setup and loop functions.

Inside the setup function, you will set each of the pins to output. Then, you will turn green

```
int green = 2; //LED3
int yellow = 3; //LED2
int red = 4; //LED1

void setup() {
    pinMode(green, OUTPUT);
    pinMode(yellow, OUTPUT);
    pinMode(red, OUTPUT);

    digitalWrite(green, LOW);
    digitalWrite(yellow, LOW);
    digitalWrite(red, HIGH);
}
```

and yellow off (low) and red on (high).

Inside the loop function you will start by delaying 5 seconds. This will be for the red light. Second, you will turn red off and green on and delay 5 seconds for the green light. Third, you will turn green off and yellow on and delay 2 seconds for the yellow light. Fourth, you will turn yellow off

```
void loop() {
    delay(5000); //red light
    digitalWrite(red, LOW);
    digitalWrite(green, HIGH);
    delay(5000); //green light
    digitalWrite(green, LOW);
    digitalWrite(yellow, HIGH);
    delay(2000); //yellow light
    digitalWrite(yellow, LOW);
    digitalWrite(red, HIGH);
}
```

and red on. Since the loop function will be repeated, the delay for the next red light is the one at the beginning of the loop function.

Activity 2 - Four- Way Traffic Signal

Overview

Figure 3a shows a simple road intersection with a traffic signal. Each side of this intersection has one set of lights (red, yellow, and green). For this activity, you are going to simulate the lights at this intersection with the Arduino. You can use concepts from the last assignment to further your design into a 4-way traffic signal.

The general idea will be that when one direction (two lights) is green, the other direction (two lights) is red. Example light colors are shown in figure 3b.

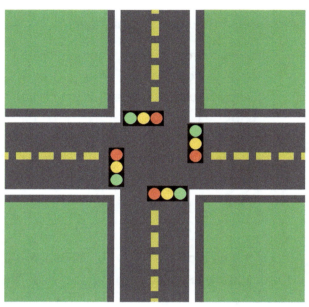

Figure 3a – Four-Way Signal

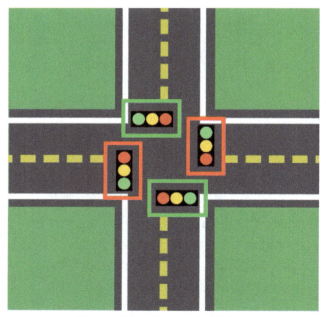

Figure 3b – Example Lights

You will use the same timing of 5 seconds for red, 5 seconds for green, and 2 seconds for yellow. One change to this is that you should add in one second where both lights are red. This is called the "all-red clearance interval" and is used to ensure the intersection is cleared of traffic before changing a different side of the signal to green.

Breadboard

For this circuit, it is easier to visualize the circuit by looking at the breadboard image first. If you think of your breadboard like a road, you can lay out our traffic signal LEDs in much the same way.

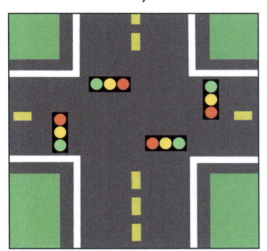 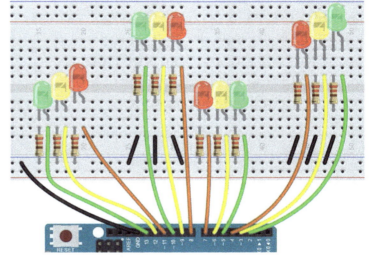

Schematic

Here is the schematic for the circuit. Each LED is labeled with its color and they are grouped in threes for each direction.

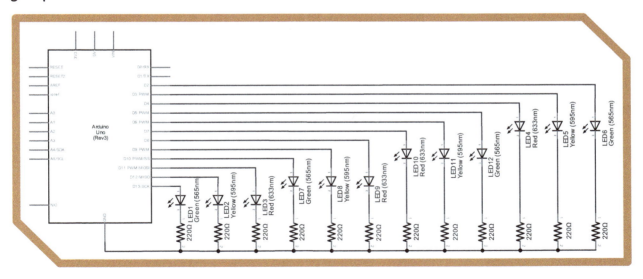

Code

For this program, I will help you get started, but you will be writing a lot of the code on your own. First, before the setup function, you'll use variables to hold all of our pin numbers. This will keep everything organized – it makes it much easier to figure out which pin is which. I have labeled all of them with comments of the names that match the schematic.

Your setup function needs to contain the following:

- Initialize all your pins to output
- Turn all the red lights on
- Turn all the yellow and green lights off

This will begin your program at the one second of all red lights.

```
int red_1 = 4;  //LED4
int yellow_1 = 3;  //LED5
int green_1 = 2;  //LED6

int red_2 = 7;  //LED10
int yellow_2 = 6;  //LED11
int green_2 = 5;  //LED12

int red_3 = 8;  //LED9
int yellow_3 = 9;  //LED8
int green_3 = 10;  //LED7

int red_4 = 11;  //LED3
int yellow_4 = 12;  //LED2
int green_4 = 13;  //LED1
```

The loop function for this activity follows a very similar method as the first activity. You will use delay functions for timing. You will turn lights on and off to follow the appropriate cycle. Remember, lights will operate in pairs so you for each on and off, you will be cycling two lights instead of just one. Because there are two directions, you will have two different green/yellow cycles (one for each direction) in your loop.

Conclusion

Hopefully these assignments have given you some good practice with programming and building circuits. The next lesson will introduce a couple new programming concepts as well as practicing what you have learned some more. You will also use a couple new electronic components.

The full code for activity 2 is in the solutions section at the back of the book.

Lesson 4 - Decisions and Noises

Making Decisions - The if/else statement

This activities in this lesson will use a new type of programming – decision structures. So far, you have been using sequential programming where the code is just executed one line at a time in order. Decision structures allow the computer to pick from multiple choices of which code to execute based on certain conditions.

The first decision structure you will use is the if-else statement. The general form of an if-else statement looks like this:

```
if(condition){
    // if condition is true
}
else{
    // if condition is false
}
```

The if statement will contain a condition in parentheses. If the condition is true, the code inside the curly braces will be executed. After that is the else statement which will be executed if the condition is false. In any case, whenever your Arduino reaches an if-else statement, only one of the statements will be executed, either if or else.

For the condition of an if statement, you have a few options. The condition will always be a statement that executes to be true or false. This could involve numerical values, input from pin readings, etc. These values will then be compared to other numerical values, or the values high or low, to determine whether a condition is true. Comparison operators are used for this.

Comparison operators are used to compare two values. These include the following:

- == – equal to (Note: this is two equal signs. Using only one – the assignment operator – will produce incorrect results in a comparison.)
- != – not equal to
- < – less than
- > – greater than
- <= – less than or equal to
- >= – greater than or equal to

To use these operators, one value goes on either side of the operator. Here are each of them comparing values a and b:

```
a == b
a != b
a < b
a > b
a <= b
a >= b
```

Pull-Down Resistors - A new way to use resistors

So far you have used resistors to limit current in a circuit. For this next assignment, you are going to be using resistors for a new purpose: as pull-down resistors. To explain what this means, let's look at a couple examples.

Suppose you want to connect a button to a digital pin of the Arduino to use as an input signal. It would seem that this would be an easy task, just connect a button to 5V on one side and the pin on the other side. Then, read the value from the pin to see if it is

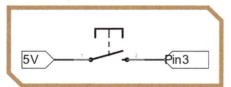

high (button pressed) or not (button not pressed). However, this doesn't quite work like you would think.

The issue with the circuit from this example is that when the button is not pressed, you end up with a pin that is not connected to anything. This is called a floating pin. In order to determine if a voltage is low or high, a pin needs a reference point. Generally the reference point is ground (low). With a floating pin, you don't have ground connected and thus no reference point. Your board can't determine if an input is high if it doesn't know what low is! This problem can be fixed by creating a reference point for the pin.

There are two ways to create a reference point – a pull-up or pull-down resistor. Throughout this book pull-down resistors are used.

New Circuit Symbol - Net Label

In the last schematic, you may have noticed a new circuit symbol. This is called a net label. Net labels are ways of labeling connections without having to draw the entire wire and can help better organize schematics. Each net label will be named and net labels that have the same name are assumed to be connected points. A full schematic will always have at least two labels with the same name (generally one connected to the board and one to a different part of the circuit). In some cases, for the simplicity of the diagram, only part of the schematic may be shown, in which case it will be assumed the other labels are connected to the board but not shown. The pins will always be labeled in such a way that it is obvious which pins on the board they are connected to.

By adding a resistor to the pin side of the button, we can ensure the pin is connected to ground, whether the button is closed or not. When the button is not pressed, the pin will be connected to ground. When the button is pressed, the current will follow the path of least resistance (this is why a fairly large value resistor is used) and the pin will read a high value.

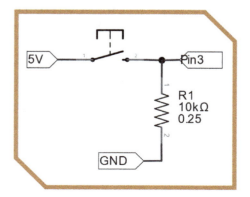

Activity 1 - Button Pushing

Overview

Let's put all the pieces together that we have been discussing. In this activity, you are going to turn an LED on and off based on button presses – turning the LED on when the button is pushed down.

Schematic

There are two pieces to this circuit – the LED and the button. The LED will be connected with a current limiting resistor on pin 2, just as in previous lessons. The button will be connected to pin 3 with a pull–down resistor as shown in the pull–down resistor example.

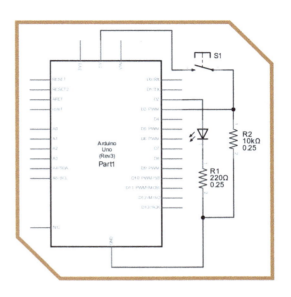

Breadboard

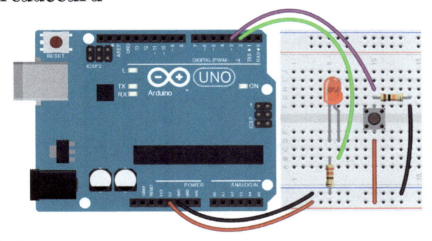

Code

Before writing code, let's consider what the program needs.

What is in the setup function?

- Initialize pin 2 (LED) to output and pin 3 (button) to input.

What is in the loop function?

- Use an if–else statement to turn the LED on.
- If the button is pushed, turn on the LED.
- Otherwise, turn off the LED.
- To determine the button pin's value, use the digitalRead function.

31

The code for this program is provided below.

```
void setup() {
  pinMode(2, OUTPUT);
  pinMode(3, INPUT);
}

void loop() {
  if(digitalRead(3) == HIGH){
    digitalWrite(2, HIGH);
  }
  else{
    digitalWrite(2, LOW);
  }
}
```

Buzz Buzz - Using Piezo Buzzers

Next up, a new component, the piezoelectric speaker, or piezo buzzer. Piezo buzzers are output devices that use a special piezoelectric material that gets electrically vibrated along with other components to help this vibration resonate to produce an audible sound. Different tones can be produced by adjusting the frequency (how many sound waves pass a point in a given amount of time – basically the speed of the sound waves) of the electric input.

Piezo buzzers have two leads. One will connect to a digital pin and the other will connect to ground. They are nonpolarized and can thus be connected either way (though the breadboard image does color the leads red and black so included images will match those colors to power and ground).

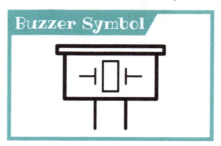

Buzzer Symbol

Controlling a Piezo Buzzer

The tone Function

Arduino provides a couple built-in functions for

`tone(pinNum, frequency, duration);`

controlling piezo buzzers. First up is the tone function. The tone function provides a given frequency to a specified pin to produce a sound on a piezo buzzer. The tone function takes two or three arguments. The first is the pin number (can be any digital pin). The second is the frequency. The third is an optional duration. If this is not included, the tone will continue until told to stop. In this lesson you will not be using this third argument.

The noTone Function

To stop a tone, you can use the noTone function. It takes one argument, the pin number in which to stop the tone (the pin the buzzer is connected to).

```
noTone(pinNum);
```

What Frequency to Use?

Frequency is measured in Hertz (Hz), or cycles per second. The tone function can output frequencies from 31 Hz to 65,535 Hz. Humans can hear an approximate range of 20 Hz to 20,000 Hz. Musical notes each have an associated frequency and you will be using some of these as you use piezo buzzers.

Activity 2 - Button Buzzer

Overview

For this activity, you will be trying out the tone and noTone functions. The goal is to play a sound on the buzzer when a button is pressed.

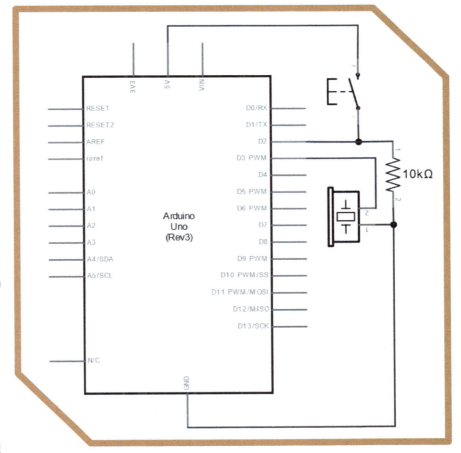

Schematic

This circuit has two main parts – the button and the buzzer. The button uses a pull-down resistor so one side is connected to 5V and the other side is connected to pin 2 and the resistor. The other side of the resistor is connected to ground. The buzzer is connected to pin 3 on one side and ground on the other side.

Breadboard

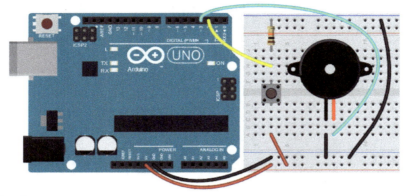

Code

The code for this program is pretty simple so the code is included here – as the programs start to get more complicated and you have had more practice, code outlines will be provided in the lessons but full code will be in the solutions section at the back of the book.

The setup function initializes pin 2 to input and pin 3 to output. The loop function has a single if/else statement. The if statement checks to see if the button is pressed. If it is, play a tone on pin 3, otherwise use the noTone function to turn the tone off.

```
void setup() {
  pinMode(2, INPUT);
  pinMode(3, OUTPUT);
}

void loop() {
  if(digitalRead(2) == HIGH){
    tone(3, 440);
  }
  else{
    noTone(3);
  }
}
```

Bonus Activity

The code is written with a frequency of 440 Hz, which is the A above middle C. Try out a few different frequencies to see what they sound like.

Conclusion

In this lesson you learned some new circuit topics: Buttons and pull–down resistors and Piezo buzzers.

And some new coding topics: If/else statements and The tone and noTone functions.

In the next lesson you will continue to practice using buzzers, learning some new coding along the way.

Lesson 5 - Making Music

Arrays - What if you need lots of variables?

Arrays are a special type of variable that can hold multiple values. There are a few ways to create arrays, but for now you will look at declaring an "array literal." To declare an array start by declaring a type (the type of items it will hold). Then name it and include a set of square brackets (this is what tells the Arduino it is an array). You can then set it equal to its value which will be a comma separated list of items enclosed in curly braces.

```
int myArray[] = {1, 2, 3, 4, 5};
```

Accessing Array Elements

```
int myArray[] = {12, 56, 37, 14, 32};
myArray[0]; //element value: 12
myArray[1]; //element value: 56
myArray[2]; //element value: 37
myArray[3]; //element value: 14
myArray[4]; //element value: 32
```

Each item in an array is called an element. You can access an element by calling its "index" which is just its position number. The first element will always have an index of 0. We call an index by writing the name of the array followed by square brackets that contain the index number. These elements can then be used just as any variable.

Using Arrays

Here is a simple example of how you can use an array. This example adds the array elements together. Array elements can be used much like any other variable, but as you will see later, there are advantages to using them if you have several values that can be grouped.

```
int numArray[] = {5, 9, 3};
int arraySum = numArray[0] + numArray[1] + numArray[2]; //17
```

Loop-de-Loops - For Loops

Suppose you have a section of code that you want to execute a specific number of times. You can use a for loop to accomplish this. For

```
for(statement1; statement2; statement3){

}
```

loops have three specifier statements: a start point, a condition, and an increment. These statements are separated by semicolons.

For Loop Start Point

The first specifier of a for loop is the start point. This is declared as an integer variable and given a value. For example: int i = 0 will begin the for loop at 0. (Note: i is a common variable name that is used in for loops.) Replacing this in the example:

```
for(int i = 0; statement2; statement3){

}
```

For Loop Condition

The second specifier in a for loop is the condition. This determines the end point of the loop and will contain the defined variable, a conditional operator (==, <, >, <=, >=), and a comparison value. The loop will execute until the condition is no longer true. For example: i < 10 means the loop will execute until i is no longer less than 10. Replacing this in the example:

```
for(int i = 0; i < 10; statement3){

}
```

For Loop Increment

The third specifier in a for loop is the increment. The value of the variable needs to be reassigned as an incremented value of itself – either up or down. This is the equation the loop will use to recalculate the variable used in the condition to determine if the loop should keep going. For example: i = i + 1 (Note: There is another way to write this equation. For an increment of 1 you can use an increment operator, ++. This operator can be used with a variable name to increment an integer by 1, so writing i++ is the same as writing i = i + 1.) Replacing in the example:

```
for(int i = 0; i < 10; i=i+1){

}
```

```
for(int i = 0; i < 10; i++){

}
```

Putting it all Together

In the final for loop example, the for loop begins at 0, increments by 1, and ends at 9. Therefore, it will loop 10 times (0–9). The variable, i, while controlling the loop can also be used inside the loop, such as when indexing an array. This can be useful if you need to loop through an array such as in the following example. This example shows how you might use a for loop to access each of the elements of an array and assign them to a variable named x.

```
int myArray[] = {22, 11, 53, 5, 6, 53, 7, 8, 40, 34};
for(int i = 0; i < 10; i++){
    int x = myArray[i];
}
```

More Decisions - An extension on the if and else statements

```
if(condition){
   // if condition is true
}
else{
   // if condition is false
}
```

You previously learned about the if and else statements. These allow you to make a choice based on a condition – either the condition is met and the if statement is executed, or the condition is not met and the else statement is executed.

Else If Statements

What if you want to have multiple options when checking conditions? That is where the else if statement comes in. You can use it to add additional conditions to an if/else decision structure. The processor will check each condition, starting at the beginning. If it finds a true condition, that statement's code will execute and the processor will ignore any

```
if(condition1){
   // if condition1 is true
}
else if(condition2){
   // if condition2 is true
}
else{
   // if both conditions are false
}
```

following statements that are part of the set of statements and move onto the next part of the code.

Activity - Mini Piano

Overview

This program will build on the last lesson where you used a piezo buzzer, to build a mini piano. This will be a piano with 8 keys and you will set it to play the C major scale, starting at middle C. The tone function can only play a single frequency at a time, so you will only be able to play one note at a time. The schematic is large but is just 8 buttons (with pull-down resistors) on pins 2–9 and the buzzer on pin 10.

Schematic

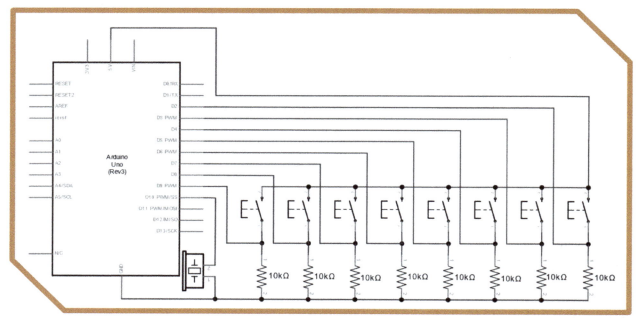

Breadboard

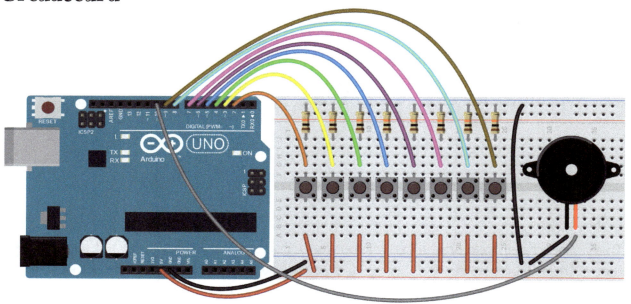

Code

For this activity, the pseudocode is included below to guide you through writing the code yourself. (Note: Pseudocode is a way of outlining a program in detail without writing its exact syntax.) Before the setup function you are going to create integer variables to hold the frequency values for each of the notes. The rest of the pseudocode is listed below.

- Before Setup function:
    - Optional – create a variable for your buzzer pin. You may want to include this if you find reading variable names easier than reading pin numbers.
    - Create the following integer variables for the notes of your scale:

```
int c1 = 262;
int d = 294;
int e = 330;
int f = 349;
int g = 392;
int a = 440;
int b = 494;
int c2 = 523;
```

- Setup function:
    - Use a for loop to initialize pins 2 to 9 as input.
    - Initialize pin 10 as output.
- Loop function:
    - Create 8 integer variables to digitalRead each button.
    - Use an if/else if/else statement to check if each value is high.
        - The if/else if statements which are checking each button should each contain a tone function which plays the corresponding note.
        - The else statement should contain the noTone function.

Bonus Activity #1

Instead of using 8 different variables to read your button values, use an array so that you can read the values with an array. You will probably want to create the array before the setup function. It may take a bit of thinking to figure out how to write the for loop to both index with 0–7 and read pins 2–9. There a couple options for how to do this.

Bonus Activity #2

There is a list of notes and their frequencies in the references section at the back of the book. Try using a different scale/set of notes for your buttons. There is also a list of the major scales.

Conclusion

In this lesson you learned some new coding concepts: else if statements, arrays, and for loops. In the next lesson, you will be practicing these concepts and building upon them a bit more to continue developing your programming skills.

Lesson 6a - Rolling the Dice (Part 1)

Decisions...Decisions... – The Switch Statement

So far in decision making, you have used if, else if, and else statements. These work well for many types of decisions but can at times be a bit cumbersome. In cases where you just need to check for a variable being a certain value, you have another option.

The switch statement takes a single variable and compares its value against a list of values. There are a few types that the variable can be, but for now we will only look at integers. If the value of the variable matches one of the cases in the statement, it executes the code in that section. If not, a default section can be included at the end to execute instead.

Shown here is the general format of the switch statement. The variable to compare is in parentheses after the word switch. The cases (possible variable values) are included in a set of curly braces following. Each case is specified by writing case and the comparison value followed by a colon.

```
switch(variable){
  case 1:
    //some code goes here
    break;
  case 2:
    //some code goes here
    break;
  case 3:
    //some code goes here
    break;
  default:
    //some code goes here
    break;
}
```

Within each case, code is written to be executed when that case occurs (like the code that would be inside an if or else if statement). This block is usually indented for clarity.

At the end of each case, include the keyword break (followed by a semi-colon). This exits the switch statement. Without this, the Arduino will execute the entire rest of the switch statement, whether there are more cases or not.

The default case is like an else statement. This will be executed for any value and is what will execute if none of the other cases are true. A default case is not required in a switch statement.

While...While...While - Using While Loops

Suppose you want to loop through a certain set of code a few times. Maybe until something specific happens or while something is true. This is where you will use something called while loops. A while loop will continue to execute while a specified condition is true.

```
while(condition){
   //code in here will execute as long as the condition is true
}
```

As an example, suppose a while loop needs to execute until a variable, myVar, is equal to 10 or "while myVar is less than 10." The condition is checked before each execution of the loop. The loop will execute as long as the condition is true. This loop will execute 10 times: while myVar equals 0, 1, 2, 3, 4, 5, 6, 7, 8, and 9. Since the condition is checked before execution, when the loop is finished, myVar will equal 10.

```
int myVar = 0;
while(myVar < 10){
   myVar = myVar + 1;
}
```

So Random (Sort of) - The Random Function

For this lesson's assignment, you will be using a new built-in function, the random function. This function generates pseudo-random numbers. Pseudo-random numbers are simulated random numbers that are calculated mathematically using a starting value, called a seed value. The random function takes either one or two arguments to provide a range of values in which to generate numbers:

- min (optional – if not provided, range will start at 0)
- max (the range used will be max–1 so make sure to include 1 more value than you want in your range).

The random function returns a value each time it is called so you will use a variable to hold the value. Here is an example of an integer value myRandomVar which holds the

```
int myRandomVar = random(min,max);
```

value of the random function in the range min, max–1.

To further illustrate, this random function would generate a value of 1, 2, 3, 4, 5, or 6.

```
random(1,7)
```

Flagging Things - Bools and Flags

New Data Type: Bools

Boolean values, or bools, can have one of two values: true or false. These can be useful for places where you only need a variable to have two possibilities – either for comparison or for flagging. While a 0 or 1 integer value can be (and sometimes is) used for the same purpose, the advantage of Boolean values is that they take up less space in your Arduino's memory (16 bits vs. 8 bits). This is especially helpful in larger programs.

Flag Variables

Flag variables are variables that act as signals to let the program know that a certain condition has been met. Generally, they will be set to false if the condition has not been met, or true if the condition has been met. This could be reaching a certain point in a program, turning on or off components, reading a certain value from a component, etc. Since the value needs to be read through the entirety of the program, the variable will generally be initialized before the setup function.

Variable Scope

This hasn't specifically discussed yet but has been slightly addressed, so let's talk about it now – the topic of variable scope. Variable scope is where each variable can be accessed by the program. Variables are accessible wherever they are created. If they are created within a function, they can be used in that function. If they are created within a loop, they can be used in that loop. Your Arduino will automatically delete variables once they are out of scope. By declaring a variable at the beginning of a file, not inside a function, we can access that variable in the entire file – this is useful when a variable needs to be used in both the setup and loop functions.

Which Way is Up? - Tilt Switches

 Next, a new component, tilt switches. They will be used just like other switches and buttons, but they are switched on and off by physically tilting them sideways. The switch is "closed" when upright and "open" when turned sideways. In this lesson, tilt switches will be used with pull-down resistors as with buttons in previous lessons.

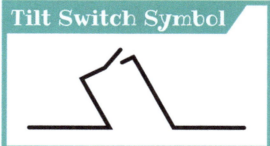
Tilt Switch Symbol

Activity - Electronic Die #1

Overview

In this assignment, you will be building an electronic die using LEDs and a tilt switch. The tilt switch will be used to represent rolling the die. There will be 7 LEDs laid out to represent the face of the die. (The positive sides of the LEDs will be connected to digital pins of the Arduino which is not shown here.)

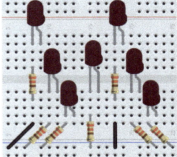

The die will be able to display the values 1–6, just like a regular 6 face game die. The LEDs would look something like this:

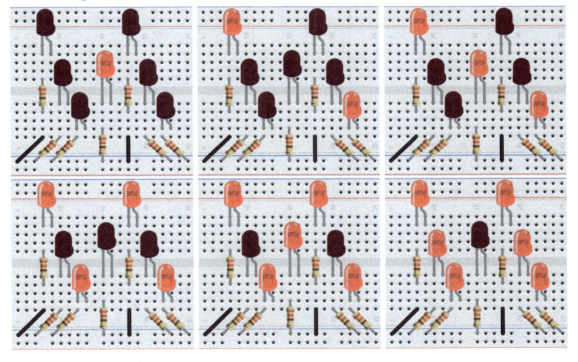

Schematic

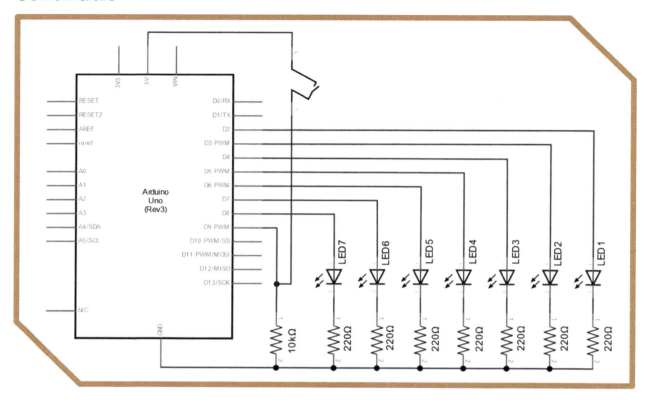

Breadboard

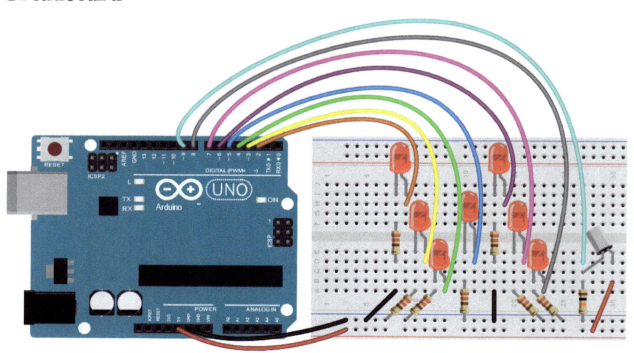

Code

Below is the pseudocode for the program. There are a few variables that you want to go ahead and initialize before the setup function, that way your program has access to them the entire time – as discussed in the previous variable scope section.

In order to use for loops for output later, you need to create arrays that have the necessary output values for each die face. Each array will have 0s and 1s to turn on and off the LEDs to display each face. Here is the layout of the LED pin numbers:

2		6
3	5	7
4		8

Within the setup function, you will initialize the pins and set their initial values.

```
• Before setup function:
    • Create variables for each pin (7 LEDs and tilt
      switch). Use an array for the LEDs.
    • Create three flag variables:
        1. rolled - indicates if die has been rolled
           (initialize to false as die has not been rolled)
        2. off - indicates if the lights are off (initialize
           to false as lights have not been set)
        3. tiltState - indicates if the switch is tilted
           (does not need an initialization value as it is
           based on the read pin value)
    • Create arrays for the LED output values for each die
      face.
    • Something like:
        int one[]   = {0,0,0,1,0,0,0};
        int two[]   = {1,0,0,0,0,0,1};
        int three[] = {1,0,0,1,0,0,1};
        int four[]  = {1,0,1,0,1,0,1};
        int five[]  = {1,0,1,1,1,0,1};
        int six[]   = {1,1,1,0,1,1,1};
• Setup function
    • Set LED pins to output (you can use a for loop for
      this)
    • Set switch pin to input
    • Turn all LEDs off (again, use a for loop)
    • Set off flag to true since all lights are now off
```

The first part of the loop function starts by reading the switch and then has a while loop that will execute when the switch is tilted (low). This while loop will ensure all the lights get turned off and the proper flag is set to signal a die roll. The loop will end once the tilt switch pin reads a high value (switch is upright)

The second part of the loop function is an if statement that contains all of the code to produce a die roll. The roll is signaled by both a flag (this makes sure the lights have been turned off inside the while loop) and the switch value. Within this statement, a random value is generated and then lights are turned on based on that value.

- Loop function
  - Read the state of the switch
  - While switch value is low (switch is tilted, thus the die is being rolled)
    - If all the lights are not off, turn them off and set off flag to true.
    - Set rolled flag to true (die has been rolled).
    - Read the state of the switch.
  - If the switch value is high (not tilted) and rolled status is 1 (die has been rolled):
    - Set both rolled flag and off flag to false to reset them for the next roll.
    - Create an integer variable, dice that generates a random value from 1 to 6.
    - Use a switch statement to check for each possible value. The code for each case will contain a for loop that turns on the necessary lights.

Here is an example of one of the switch cases:

```
case 1:
  for(int i = 0; i < 7; i++){
    digitalWrite(LEDs[i],one[i]);
  }
  break;
```

Conclusion

In this lesson a new component was introduced:
- Tilt switches

You also learned a couple new coding topics:
- Switch statement
- While loops
- Random function
- Flag variables

You are going to be returning to this project in the next lesson, so make sure you save your code.

Lesson 6b - Rolling the Dice (Part 2)

Review

In the last lesson, you built an electronic die using LEDs, using a tilt switch to simulate rolling the die.

You learned a few new coding topics:
- While Loops
- Random function
- Flag variables

In this lesson, you will be recreating that circuit with a seven-segment display.

Displaying Numbers - Using Seven-Segment Displays

You are most likely familiar with a seven-segment display whether you know what it is called, or not. It is the display seen in most digital clocks. It has 7 segments which are individual lights. Therefore, these lights can be turned on and off by sending high or low signals to each one, just like you have done with LEDs. The hardest part of using one is figuring out which pins are which and which ones to turn on for each digit, which may just take some playing around with.

Here is the breadboard image for the seven-segment display. The pins are marked as to what segment they are. Your actual component may not have these markings but the pins should be in the same order. As you can see, it has an eighth segment, the period. Since you aren't using this for this lesson, you do not need to connect this pin. There are also two ground pins (the middle pins on both top and bottom), which are connected together. Only one of them needs to be connected to ground of the Arduino.

As seen in the schematic image, each pin is just a separate LED and in the image is labeled according to which segment it is. The top pin is the ground pin.

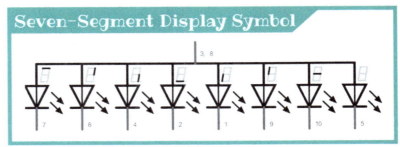

Seven-Segment Display Symbol

This is how a seven-segment display will be set up on a breadboard.

A couple notes:

- Each segment is connected to power in this example, but would normally be connected to digital pins on the Arduino.
- A 220 ohm resistor is placed on each segment to limit current.
- The decimal point is not connected since it is not needed in this lesson, but it could be connected just like the other segments.
- You only need to connect one of the ground pins to ground as they are tied together within the display.

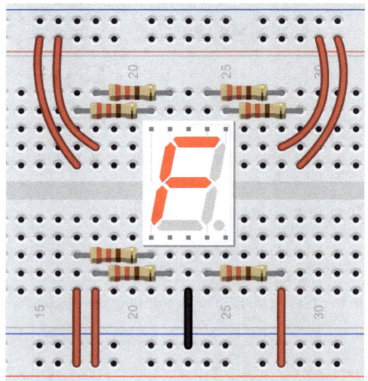

Below are examples of how to display the numbers 1 to 6 on a seven-segment display:

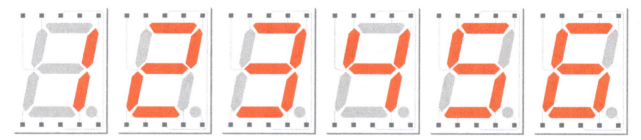

Activity - Electronic Die #2

Overview

Just like in the last lesson, you will be building an electronic die. Instead of the 7 LEDs, you will be using a seven-segment display.

Schematic

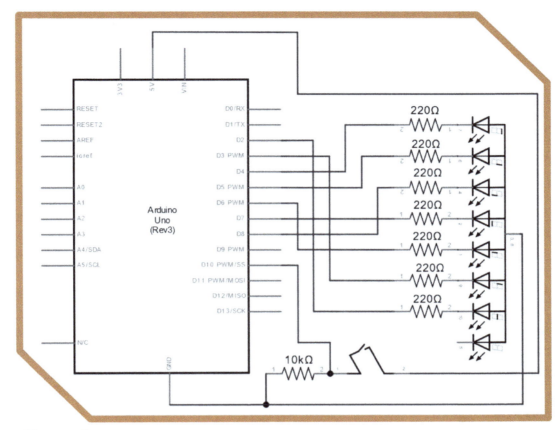

Breadboard

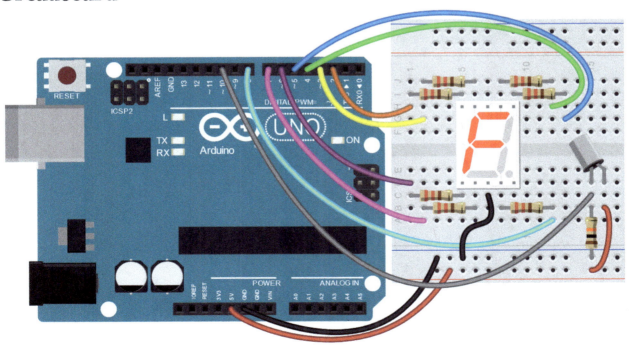

Code

```
Seven-segment
  pin layout:
        4
    3       5
        2
    6       8
        7
```

The only difference from the last (LED) version of the electronic die to the seven-segment version is the order of the pins and the necessary output to each of them. As long as your display is connected as in the pin layout diagram shown here, these example arrays will turn on and off the proper lights to display each of the numbers 1–6 using their corresponding arrays.

```
int one[]   = {0,0,0,1,0,0,1};
int two[]   = {1,0,1,1,1,1,0};
int three[] = {1,0,1,1,0,1,1};
int four[]  = {1,1,0,1,0,0,1};
int five[]  = {1,1,1,0,0,1,1};
int six[]   = {1,1,1,0,1,1,1};
```

Refer to the previous lesson for the pseudocode as needed.

Conclusion

In this lesson a new component was introduced – the seven-segment display. You also practiced coding concepts learned in the last couple lessons. Make sure to save your code from this activity so you can reuse your output arrays for the seven-segment display (if you connect it the same way in future lessons, you don't have to figure out the number outputs again).

Lesson 7 - Going Analog

Digital vs. Analog - What are Signals Anyway?

Digital Signals

So far, you have been using digital signals with all your components. Digital signals work in "discrete" values, like flat steps. For example, all of the code so far has used a high or low value, so values of 0 or 1. On a graph, that would look something like this:

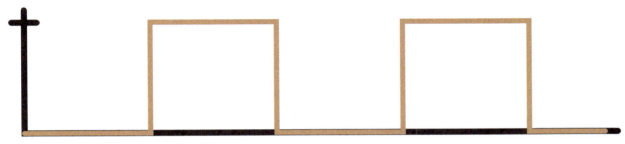

Analog Signals

In this lesson, analog components will be introduced, which produce an analog signal, rather than digital. Analog signals produce a continuous range of values instead of distinct steps and are read through the Arduino's analog pins. An analog signal might look something like the following:

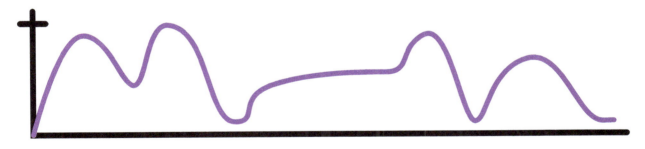

What is a Signal Anyway?

Let's pause for a minute and discuss what a signal actually is – rather, what your Arduino is measuring when it is getting an input signal. The Arduino Uno that you use is generally using a voltage of 5 V. Really, what your Arduino is reading when reading an input value is a voltage. For digital input signals, it interprets the voltage read as either a high or low value (the voltage needs to be at least 3 V to be considered high). Since analog components produce a more varying signal, the signal read will be somewhere in between 0 V and 5 V.

Analog to Digital Conversion

Your Arduino takes analog input through its analog pins. However, your Arduino can only really operate on values in digital. Therefore, it must convert this signal into a digital signal. Since it expects a voltage between 0V and 5 V, it takes this range and converts it to digital by dividing it into 1024 distinct steps (10 bits). Here is a very simplified view of what analog to digital conversion
might look like for a given signal:

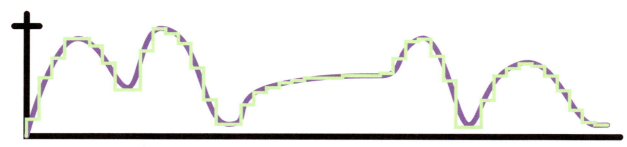

Getting Analog Input

`analogRead(analogPinNum)` Analog input is read using the analogRead function which takes one argument, a pin number (must be an analog pin). Analog pins do not need to be initialized using the pinMode function.

Modifying Resistance - Using Potentiometers

Potentiometers are "variable resistors." (Sometimes the name is shortened to pot.) They are components that allow you to manually move a sliding terminal across a resistive material. The ones you will use are called single-turn rotary pots. By rotating the rotary portion of the pot, the resistance can be adjusted from 0 ohms up to a certain value (the ones used here will be 10,000 ohms or 10k ohms).

Before getting too in depth about how pots work, let's look at the breadboard and schematic images. Potentiometers have 3 pins. The bottom two connect to power and ground. The top one will connect to your analog pin as this is where the changing resistance values can be observed.

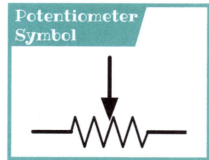

Potentiometer Symbol

The Theory of Potentiometers

The changing resistance of a potentiometer allows it to output different voltages – which is what the analog pins on the Arduino reads as different values. This is because a potentiometer is creating what is called a voltage divider. Here is a simple example voltage divider circuit:

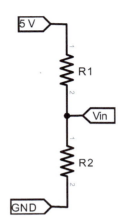

The equation of a voltage divider is as follows:

$$\text{Vin} = 5\text{V} \times \frac{R2}{R1 + R2}$$

Voltage Divider Examples

The potentiometers you are using are 10000 ohms. Since a pot is a single resistive device, R1 + R2 will always equal 10000. The only thing you are changing by rotating the pot is the ratio of R1 and R2. As a first example, suppose R1 = R2 = 5000 ohms.

$$\text{Vin} = 5 \times \frac{5000}{5000 + 5000} = 2.5\text{ V}$$

The voltage produced is 2.5 V which makes sense because it is half of 5 V and the resistance was split in half. The voltages will be directly (linearly) proportional to the resistances.

Looking at R1 = 25% of the total resistance (2500 ohms):

$$\text{Vin} = 5 \times \frac{7500}{2500 + 7500} = 3.75\text{ V}$$

And, R1 = 75% of the total resistance (7500 ohms):

$$\text{Vin} = 5 \times \frac{2500}{7500 + 2500} = 1.25\text{ V}$$

Map Function - Mapping Ranges of Values

For the assignments in this lesson, you will be using a new built-in function, the map function. This function allows you to "map" a range of values to a different range of values, essentially converting a range into a new range. Before looking at the math, let's look at the general form of this function.

```
map(value, fromLow, fromHigh, toLow, toHigh);
```

- value is the value to be converted (from the original range to a new range)
- fromLow and fromHigh are the low and high values of the original range
- toLow and toHigh are the low and high values of the new range

Basics of Number Conversions

Suppose you have a value of 12 ft that you wish to convert to meters. The conversion factor for this is 0.3048 m = 1 ft. You can create a ratio from your conversion factor and multiply it by your original value to convert it to the new value:

** Units on the top of a fraction will cancel with units on the bottom of that fraction.

$$12 \,\cancel{ft} \times \frac{0.3048 \text{ m}}{1 \,\cancel{ft}} = 3.658 \text{ m}$$

The Math Behind the Map Function

Here is the actual code for the map function:

```
long map(long x, long in_min, long in_max, long out_min, long out_max) {
   return (x - in_min) * (out_max - out_min) / (in_max - in_min) + out_min;
}
```

Let's make the math a little clearer by writing it as a fraction:

$$(x - in_{min}) \times \frac{(out_{max} - out_{min})}{(in_{max} - in_{min})} + out_{min}$$

As an example, suppose you want to convert a value of 50 from a range of 0–100 to a range of 0–200. Putting these values to their corresponding variables:

- x = 50
- in_{min} = 0
- in_{max} = 100
- out_{min} = 0
- out_{max} = 200

Substituting the values:

$$(x - in_{min}) \times \frac{(out_{max} - out_{min})}{(in_{max} - in_{min})} + out_{min}$$

$$(50 - 0) \times \frac{(200 - 0)}{(100 - 0)} + 0$$

$$50 \times \frac{200}{100}$$

$$100$$

Looking at the final equation just before solving: $50 \times \frac{200}{100}$

This equation looks just like the conversion equation – a value multiplied by a ratio of the new to the old. The only difference between this simplified version and the original $((x - in_{min}) \times \frac{(out_{max} - out_{min})}{(in_{max} - in_{min})} + out_{min})$ is that the original adds in the minimum values to account for the ranges not necessarily beginning at 0. Since the ranges in our example both began at 0, these added values "go away."

54

To conclude, all the map function is doing is creating a ratio conversion between two number ranges. This is often called "linear interpolation." This will work for any two ranges of values. One limitation with the map function that should be noted is that it works with integer math, meaning that it will only produce integer results (no decimal places). Normally, this doesn't affect things too much but can cause slight issues in cases of small ranges. The reason for this being the case is that integer operations are much faster to perform than floating point (decimal) operations.

Activity 1 - Buzzing About

Overview

The goal of this assignment is to practice using a potentiometer for analog input and the map function. You will be using a potentiometer to control the frequency of a piezo buzzer.

Schematic

In this circuit, the buzzer will get connected to pin 2 and ground just like the last lesson. The potentiometer will get connected to 5V, pin A0, and ground.

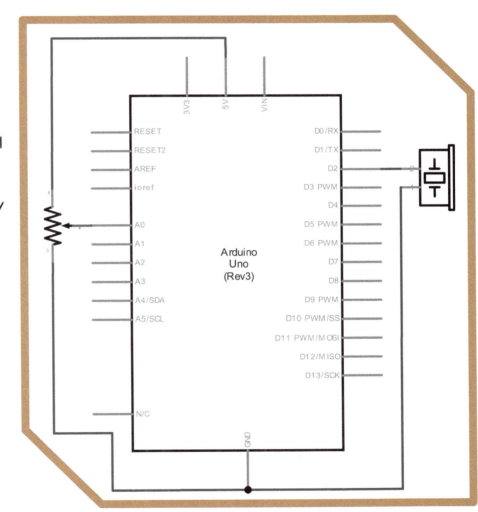

Breadboard

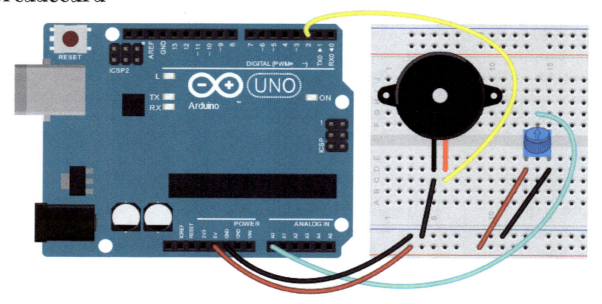

Code

The code for this program is very simple, so it has been included in full here.

In the setup function, pin 2 needs to be set to OUTPUT.

In the loop function:

```
void setup() {
   pinMode(2,OUTPUT);
}
```

- Create a variable to hold the frequency value.
  This value is determined by the map function.
- The map function arguments are as follows:
    - Value to convert: analogRead(A0) (reading from the potentiometer)
    - Original range of values: 0–1023 (the range of possible values from the potentiometer)
    - New Range: 31–5000 (range of frequencies for the buzzer – this range was picked based on the lowest possible output and approximate upper limit of human hearing)
- Once calculated, the frequency can be used in the tone function which will play it on the buzzer.

```
void loop() {
   int freqVal = map(analogRead(A0),0,1023,31,5000);
   tone(2,freqVal);
}
```

Pulse Width Modulation - Making Digital Go Analog

While you do not have the ability to output an analog signal from the Arduino, you can simulate one using pulse width modulation.

Normally, when a digital output signal is high, it remains at a steady value, something like this:

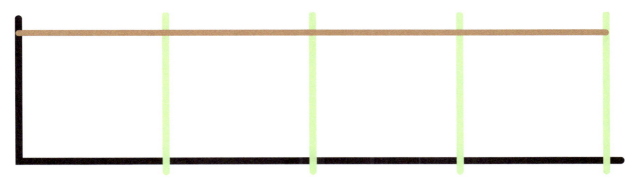

Pulse width modulation simulates an analog signal by turning the output signal on and off over given intervals of time. This gives the illusion of a lower voltage output. For example, to simulate 2.5 V output, the Arduino can turn off the signal for half of each time interval (since digital pins output 5 V), something like this:

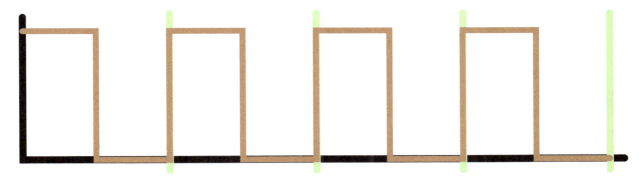

The amount that the signal is turned on and off is measured in percentages. This is called duty cycle, and it is referred to based on what percentage of the interval the signal is high. Here are examples of 100, 75, 50, and 25 percent. This would simulate voltages of 5 V, 3.75 V, 2.5 V, and 1.25 V

```
analogWrite(PWMPinNum,PWMVal);
```
On the Arduino Uno, there are 6 digital pins that support the use of PWM: 3, 5, 6, 9, 10, and 11. They are marked with the tilde symbol (~). The PWM signal uses 8 bits and thus is broken into 256 steps, numbered 0–255. These are the output values you can use. As an example, a 50% duty cycle would correspond to 50% of this range, so an output value of 127. To use PWM, initialize a PWM pin to OUTPUT mode and then you can call the function analogWrite which takes two arguments, the pin number, and the value.

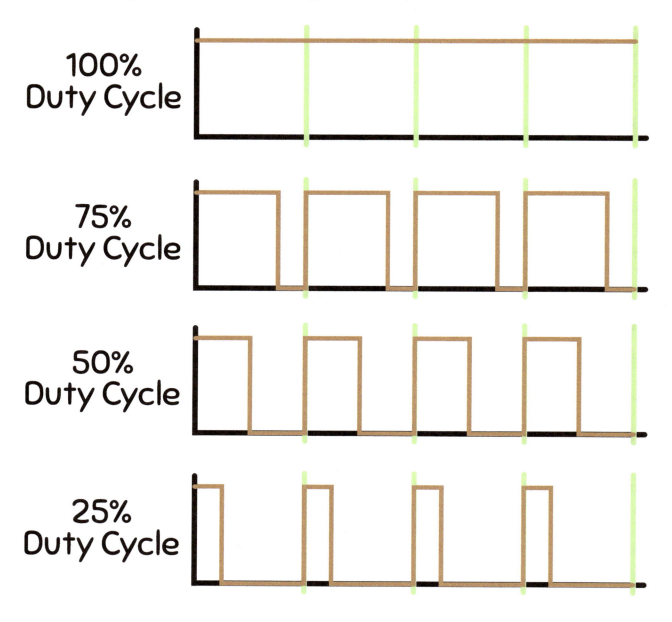

100% Duty Cycle

75% Duty Cycle

50% Duty Cycle

25% Duty Cycle

Multicolored Fun - Using RGB LEDs

LED Brightness and PWM

Before discussing the next component, let's pause and talk about LED brightness. In general, LED brightness can be controlled by changing how much current goes through the LED. On Arduino, you can use PWM to simulate this change. PWM will rapidly turn on and off the LED for a certain amount of time in intervals. Because this is so fast, our eyes still perceive the LED as being on constantly. However, the longer the LED is on, the brighter it appears. Thus, an LED with a 75% duty cycle will appear to be brighter than an LED with a 25% duty cycle.

New Component: RGB LED

In the next activity, you will be using a new component, an RGB LED. This is a special kind of LED that can produce any color. It has 3 input pins: red, green, and blue, which are considered the primary colors of light. Each input pin controls one color inside of the single LED. Therefore, the brightness on each can be adjusted using PWM to combine them to create any color.

On the breadboard image for the RGB LED, the pins are red, ground, green, and blue, respectively. This is what is called a common anode component, meaning the ground pin is shared by all the other pins. Each of the red, green, and blue pins will connect to a separate current-limiting resistor and then to a digital pin. The ground pin will connect to ground.

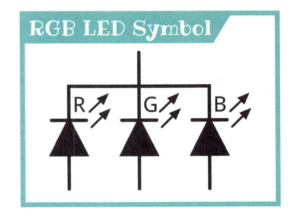

In the schematic image of the RGB LED, the ground pin is on one side and the red, green, and blue pins are labeled on the other side.

Activity 2 - Color Adjusting

Overview

In this activity, you will be using three potentiometers to control an RGB LED. The three potentiometer values will be read as analog values. These values will be converted to PWM values for each of the RGB pins of the LED.

Schematic

The circuit for this activity puts together all the pieces covered in this lesson. Potentiometers are connected to pins A0, A1, and A2 for red, green, and blue respectively. The RGB LED connects to three 220 ohm resistors that are connected to pins 9, 10, and 11 (remember, these must be PWM pins) for red, green, and blue respectively and the ground pin is connected to ground.

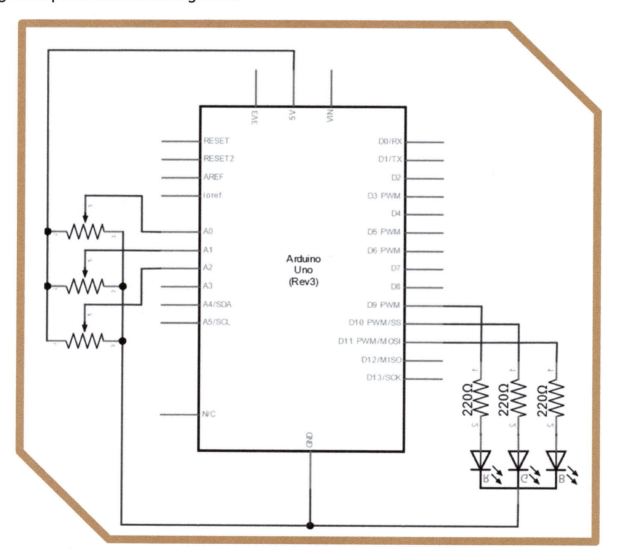

Breadboard

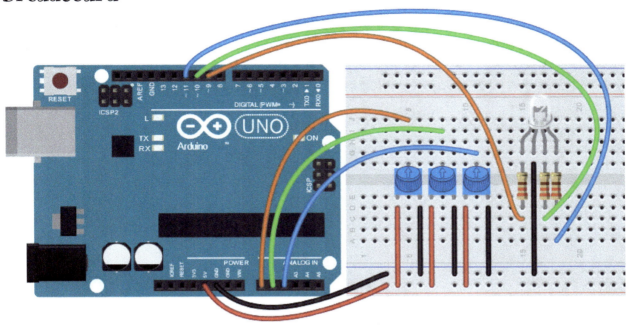

Code

Below is the pseudocode for this activity. The code will basically go through the same things three times, once for each color. So, for each line you write, you will write the same line for all three colors.

- Before setup function:
  - Create variables for each pin (3 digital and 3 analog – a red, green, and blue for each). For this assignment, I recommend using variables for pins as it will be easier to remember which is which.
- Setup function:
  - Set your 3 digital pins to output.
- Loop function:
  - Map each analog value to a PWM value. Your input value (first argument) will be an analog read of an analog pin (potentiometer value). Your two ranges will be 0-1023 and 0-255.
  - Write each value to the corresponding digital pin to output to LED.

Conclusion

In this lesson, you learned about reading analog component values through the analog pins. You also learned how to simulate analog output using pulse width modulation. Lastly, you used two new components: potentiometers and RGB LEDs. In the next lesson, you will continue your study of analog input and begin looking at some new types of sensors.

Lesson 8 - Chatty Arduinos and Light

Sensing Light - Using Photoresistors

A photoresistor is a passive input component, meaning that it doesn't send signals, but responds to external input. It is a device that has a certain resistance which changes based on ambient light levels. The maximum resistance will be at the darkest level of light and the minimum resistance will be at the brightest level of light. Here is an example of the photoresistor from Tinkercad:

The minimum and maximum resistance will depend on the specific photoresistor. For your use, you don't necessarily need to know the actual values as you will be more concerned about the values from the ADC of the Arduino (0–1023). However, depending on the light in the room you may not be able to achieve the entire range of values, so you need to figure out what values you are actually getting. We will discuss how to do this in a minute, but first let's briefly look at how to set up a photoresistor circuit.

Here are the breadboard and schematic views of photoresistors:

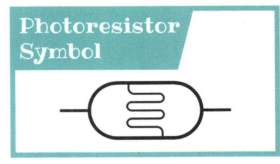

Photoresistor Symbol

To explain how to connect a photoresistor, let's first look at some ways not to connect it.

Connection to 5V and Analog Pin

The most direct way to connect a photoresistor might seem to be to connect it to 5V and an analog pin. The 5V would get lessened through the resistance of the photoresistor and the Arduino should be able to figure out what that is and convert it to a digital value. However, voltage means nothing without a reference point. (What does a high voltage mean if we have no context for low voltage?) So, the analog pin would read either only 1023 or possibly a nonsensical value.

Adding in Ground

The reference point for voltage is ground. So, let's add in ground to the circuit. This also doesn't work because now the pin is directly connected to ground and will thus always read a value of 0.

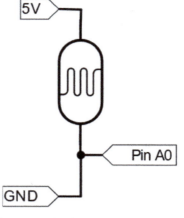

The Solution

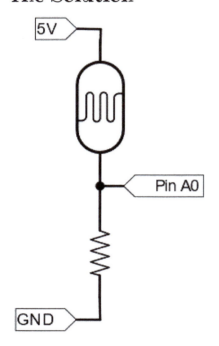

The solution to this problem is to add in a resistor between the pin and ground. This creates a voltage divider which allows your Arduino to have ground as a reference point and still be able to see a change in voltage. You could do all the calculations using the voltage divider equation but for now you'll just let the Arduino take care of that. The resistor value isn't anything super specific, but generally somewhere between 1k ohms and 10k ohms will be a good value. This will also depend on the amount of light in the room and what values you are looking for.

Let's Talk to the Arduino - The Serial Monitor

To figure out what values you are getting from your analog readings, you can use serial communication. Serial communication is the process of sending data between devices (in this case the computer and Arduino) through a communication channel (USB cord). The data is sent one bit at a time sequentially at a certain frequency.

The Arduino IDE has a built-in serial monitor which allows you to communicate with the Arduino while a program is running. You can access it by clicking the magnifying glass button in the top right corner:

The Serial Monitor will open in the bottom of the IDE window. Once you upload the program to the Arduino and it begins running, you will start seeing any specified serial communication printed in the serial monitor.

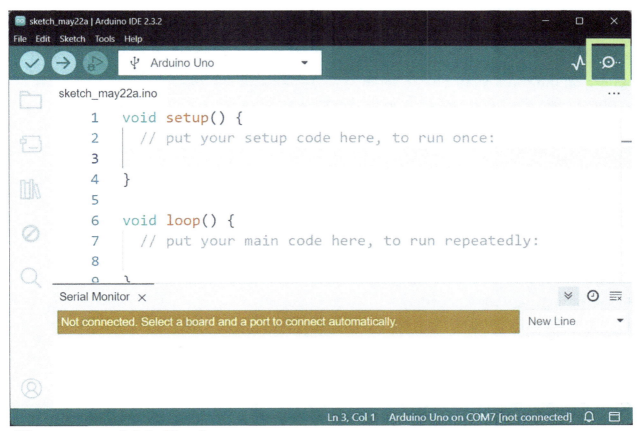

Classes and Methods

Serial is what is called a class. We won't really be discussing classes but what is important to know is that Serial is an "object" of the Serial class and it has its own set of functions that can be called. These functions are called methods and are called by writing the name of the object (Serial), a period, and the name of the function followed by parentheses that contain any arguments (if any).

```
Serial.functionName(arg);
```

To communicate with a program, first you have to start the Serial Monitor. This gets done in the setup function with the method begin. The argument in the begin method is the "baud rate" which is the frequency at which data is transmitted. For now you will use 9600. Accepted baud values are 300, 600, 1200, 2400, 4800, 9600, 14400, 19200, 28800, 31250, 38400, 57600, and 115200. The most important thing is that the serial monitor has the same rate selected as you put into the begin method.

```
Serial.begin(9600);
```

The other method you will be using is the println (short for print line) method. This will print a line of text to the serial monitor. This could be a string such as "Hello," a variable, or even an analogRead value.

```
Serial.println("Hello");
Serial.println(myVar);
Serial.println(analogRead(A0));
```

A note on the serial monitor: The serial monitor uses the TX and RX pins on the board which are connected to digital pins 0 and 1 so if you try to use these for digital input/output, you will not be able to use the serial monitor.

Activity 1 - Finding Light Levels - Using the Serial Monitor to Determine Light Levels

Overview

In this activity you will be setting up a photoresistor and reading its values using the serial monitor. Your goal is to achieve a decent range of values to use in activity 2 so try covering the photoresistor with your hand, a piece of paper, a cup, shining a flashlight on it, etc. Record some of these values and decide on a minimum and maximum value.

Schematic

Here is the schematic for the circuit. Just as discussed previously, it is a voltage divider with the photoresistor on top and a resistor on the bottom. The middle is connected to A0. This is labeled with a 10k ohm resistor, but you may want to try a few different values to see what achieves the best results.

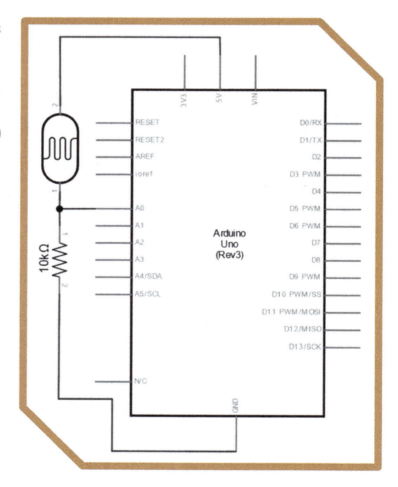

Breadboard

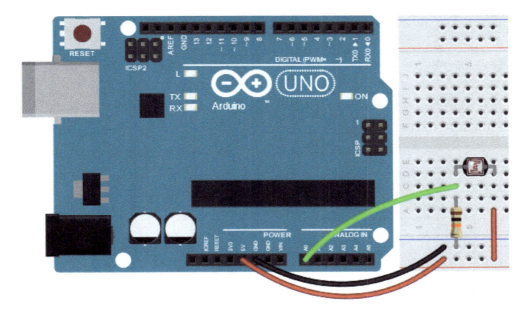

Code

The code for this activity involves starting the Serial monitor and reading the analog pin, printing the value to the Serial monitor. (Since you don't need to save this value, you can just read it inside the println method. The delay function to makes it easier to see each value.

```
void setup() {
  Serial.begin(9600);
}

void loop() {
  Serial.println(analogRead(A0));
  delay(500);
}
```

Activity 2 - Using Light Levels - Using a Photoresistor to Control Output

Overview

For this activity, you will be using the values from activity 1 to control a seven-segment display and LED. Take the minimum and maximum values and divide the range into 6 levels. Determine the minimum and maximum of each level. The range number (1-6) will be displayed on the seven-segment display. PWM will be used to adjust the brightness level of the LED dependent on the range number. Your LED PWM values are as follows: 255, 213, 171, 129, 87, 45.

Schematic

The circuit is a combination of two circuits you have built previously and the new circuit you built in activity 1:

- The seven-segment display circuit (with current-limiting resistors on each digital pin)
- An LED with current-limiting resistor (make sure it is connected to a PWM pin)
- The photoresistor circuit

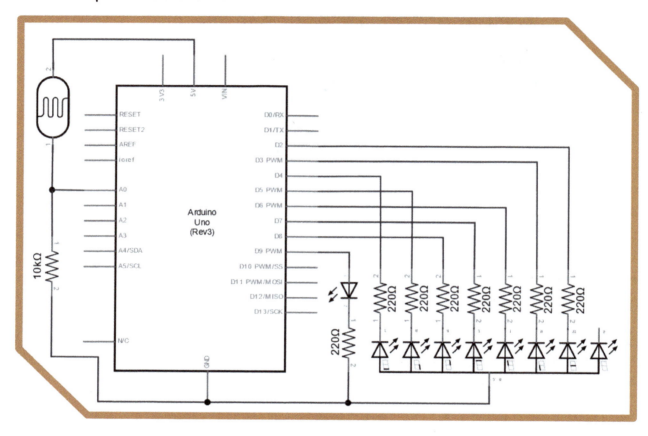

Breadboard

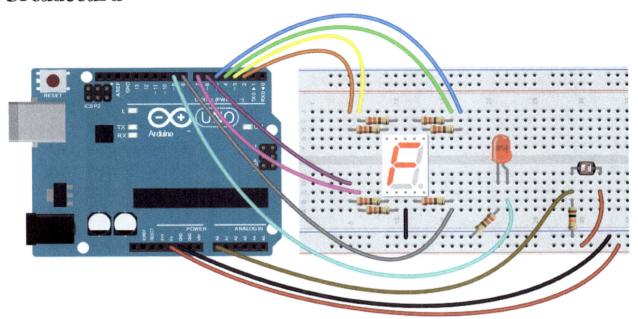

Code

Before the setup function, initialize your pins using variables. Create an array for the seven-segment display pins and arrays for the low/high values to display each digit. (This way you can just use for loops later to change the display.)

```
Sev-seg pin layout:
        4
   3         5
        2
   6         8
        7
```

```
int photo = A0;
int LED = 9;
int sevSeg[] =
{2,3,4,5,6,7,8};

int one[]   = {0,0,0,1,0,0,1};
int two[]   = {1,0,1,1,1,1,0};
int three[] = {1,0,1,1,0,1,1};
int four[]  = {1,1,0,1,0,0,1};
int five[]  = {1,1,1,0,0,1,1};
int six[]   = {1,1,1,0,1,1,1};
```

The setup function needs to contain the initialization for the digital pins. You can use a for loop for the seven segment pins (2–8). – Technically you could include pin 9 in there also since that is the LED pin. You don't need to use the Serial monitor but if you find it helpful, you could.

```
void setup() {
  for(int i = 2; i < 9; i++){
    pinMode(i, OUTPUT);
  }
  pinMode(LED, OUPUT);
}
```

The loop function starts with reading the photoresistor value. It then uses an if/else if/else statement to determine the range (1–6).

```
void loop() {
  int prVal = analogRead(photo);
  if(prVal > 800){ //6
    analogWrite(LED, 45);
    for(int i = 0; i < 8; i++){
      digitalWrite(sevSeg[i],six[i]);
    }
  }
  else if(prVal > 650){ //5
    analogWrite(LED, 87);
    for(int i = 0; i < 8; i++){
      digitalWrite(sevSeg[i],five[i]);
    }
  }
...
```

The first two are included here as an example. For each range, you need to turn on the LED to the proper level using the analogWrite function.

To display the range number on the seven segment display, you can use a for loop. A trick with if/else if statements is that your processor will always check the statements in order and execute when it finds a true condition. Therefore, you can just use greater than or equal to the minimum value of the range as the condition. For example, the value 805 will be executed by the first (if) statement because that is the first statement checked. So, the else if statement will only be values between 650 (inclusive) and 800 (non-inclusive) because anything over 800 will have already been executed by the if statement. (If the processor gets to the second statement, the condition is not satisfied in the first statement.)

Continue the if/else if/else statement for the other four ranges, using your minimum range values in the conditions. The else statement can just turn all the lights off. This would just account for a lower light condition than the lowest minimum.

Conclusion

In this lesson, you learned about photoresistors. Discussion included how they have a variable resistance based on the brightness of the light they are exposed to and how they can be read by an analog pin by using them in a voltage divider.

You also learned about the serial monitor and how it can be used to get information from the Arduino.

In the next lesson you will be learning about another type of analog sensor.

Lesson 9 - Ultrasonics
Measuring Distance with Ultrasonic Sensors

How Far Is It? - Using Ultrasonic Sensors

In this lesson, you will be using a new component, the ultrasonic sensor. This component is able to measure how far away an object is (within the range 2 cm – 400 cm). It does this by sending out a "ping" – a short sound that is a higher frequency than human hearing. If there is an object in front of the sensor, that sound will be "bounce" off the object and return to the sensor. The sensor measures how long it is between the original ping and return ping and from this the distance from the sensor to the object can be calculated.

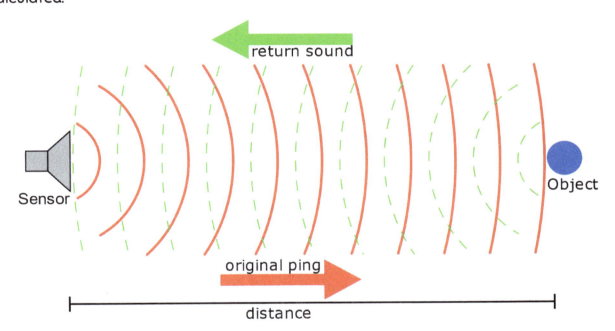

Here are the breadboard and schematic images for an ultrasonic sensor. It has 4 pins: Vcc which connects to 5V, trig and echo which both connect to digital pins, and GND which connects to ground.

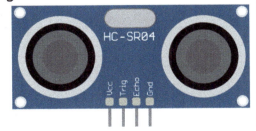

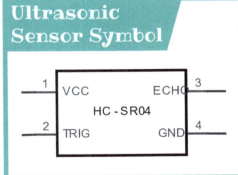

Ultrasonic Sensor Symbol

Measuring Distance - The Basics of Programming an Ultrasonic Sensor

There are two digital pins on the ultrasonic sensor. They are called trig and echo (generally called trigPin and echoPin in code). The trig pin sends out the initial ping and the echo pin measures the response time of the ping to determine how far an object is from the sensor.

Sending a Signal

A signal can be sent from the trig pin by setting it to a high value for a set length of time. Using a new built-in function, delayMicroseconds the program can be delayed by microseconds (0.000001 seconds) instead of milliseconds (0.001 seconds) that the delay function uses. The

```
digitalWrite(trigPin, LOW);
delayMicroseconds(2);

digitalWrite(trigPin, HIGH);
delayMicroseconds(10);
digitalWrite(trigPin, LOW);
```

first two lines of code set the trigPin to LOW for two microseconds to ensure that it has a low signal before sending out the "ping." The next two lines set the trigPin to HIGH for 10 microseconds which is the "ping" that the echoPin will be looking for. The last line sets the trigPin back to LOW to turn off the signal.

Reading the Signal

Once the trigPin sends a signal, the echoPin needs to look for it. This is done through the built-in function pulseIn. This function takes two arguments, a pin number that will be looking for the signal (the echo pin), and the value of the signal (either LOW or HIGH – in this case it will be HIGH). Here is the general form:

```
pulseIn(pinNum, value)
```

The pulseIn function returns the length of time it takes for the pin to receive the specified value. In this case, it records the time that it takes for the HIGH signal to return back to the echoPin after bouncing off an object.

If the echoPin does not receive a HIGH signal within 38 milliseconds, it times out, indicating that there are no objects within the readable range of the sensor. Here is an example using the pulseIn function:

```
long duration = pulseIn(echoPin, HIGH);
```

Note: we are using a new variable type here, long. This is the same as an integer but has a larger value limit.

Doing the Math

To calculate the actual distance of the object from the sensor, we can use the distance formula which says: distance = speed x time

The pulseIn function returns the time so we can multiply that by the speed, which will be the speed of sound, or 343 m/s. This converts to 0.0343 cm/microseconds. This distance then needs to be divided by 2 as the time accounts for the initial signal distance (going to the object) and the return signal distance (after bouncing off the object) – therefore by dividing by 2 we are eliminating the duplication of the distance.

We have not yet discussed how to program mathematical operations, so let's do that for just a moment. This chart shows the mathematical operators that are used in programming the Arduino. Operators follow the normal order of operations (PEMDAS) and parentheses can be used to set precedence just as in other algebraic equations. To program an equation, create an int or float variable, depending on if you need decimals or not. Then use the assignment operator (=) to set it equal to your equation. Other, already assigned variables can be used in the equation as well. Here is an example:

```
int myValue = 19;
int myAnswer = 23 * (6 + myValue); //myAnswer is 575
```

Putting the math together for the distance calculation, we arrive at the following equation to calculate the object's distance from the sensor:

```
int distance = duration * 0.0343 / 2;
```

Note: Since an integer is used to hold the result, the answer will be truncated to an integer. If you need decimal places you can use a float, but most of time rounding to the nearest cm will be fine.

Activity - Ultrasonic Alarm

Overview

This lesson's activity will be to build an ultrasonic alarm. You will be combining the ultrasonic sensor with LEDs and a buzzer to indicate when an object is too close to the sensor. Green, yellow, and red LEDs will indicate proximity ranges and the buzzer will play a tone when the red LED is illuminated. The ranges are as follows:

- Red – Object is less than or equal to 15 cm from sensor.
- Yellow – Object is greater than 15 cm and less than or equal to 30 cm from sensor.
- Green – Object is outside of those ranges.

Schematic

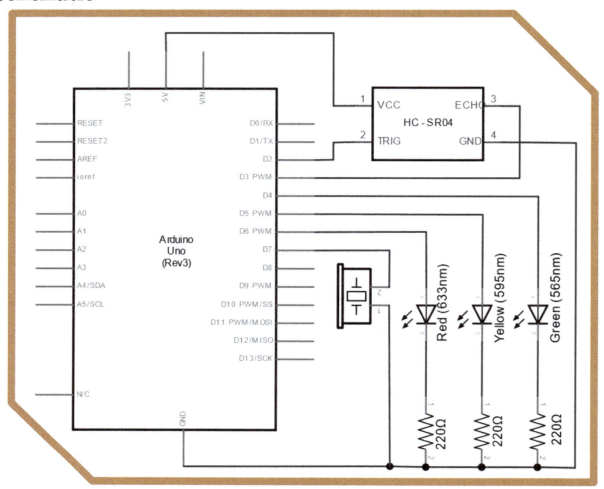

Breadboard

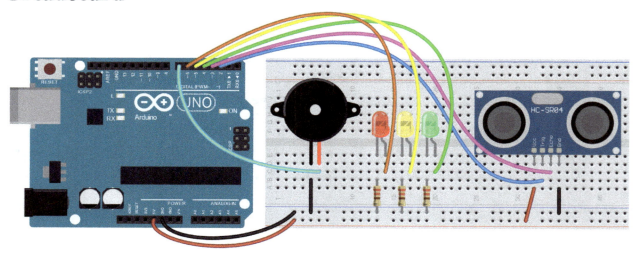

Code

For this activity mostly pseudocode is provided, aside from the ultrasonic sensor code. The rest is straightforward with turning on and off LEDs and a buzzer.

- Before setup:
  - Create integers to hold all of your pin numbers
- Setup function:
  - Set pins to INPUT/OUTPUT (echo pin will be the only input pin)
  - Turn LEDs off
- Loop function:
  - Ultrasonic sensor code:
    ```
    digitalWrite(trigPin, LOW);
    delayMicroseconds(2);

    digitalWrite(trigPin, HIGH);
    delayMicroseconds(10);
    digitalWrite(trigPin, LOW);
    long duration = pulseIn(echoPin, HIGH);
    int distance = duration * 0.0343 / 2;
    ```
  - If the distance is less than or equal to 15 cm:
    - Turn red LED on and all others off
    - Play tone on buzzer
  - Else if distance is greater than 15 cm and less than or equal to 30 cm:
    - Turn yellow LED on and all others off
    - No tone on buzzer
  - Else
    - Turn green LED on and all others off
    - No tone on buzzer

Conclusion

In this lesson, you learned to use a new component: the ultrasonic sensor. It works by sending a signal and measuring how long it takes that signal to return (if it does). This time can be used to calculate how far away an object is.

In the next lesson, you will be switching directions from the sensors you have been using and learning a new component, the LCD.

Lesson 10 - Printing Lots of Things
Using an LCD

Liquid Crystals - Displaying on an LCD

In this lesson, you will be using a new component, an LCD. LCD is short for liquid-crystal display. Liquid crystals are crystals filled with liquid that responds to electric current. They are arranged in a grid pattern along with a separate light source to display images.

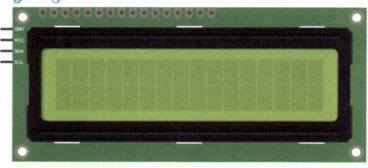

The specific LCD you are using displays characters in 2 rows of 16 columns (though the number of columns is named first, so we would say 16x2). Each character is made up of 40 pixels (5 columns x 8 rows).

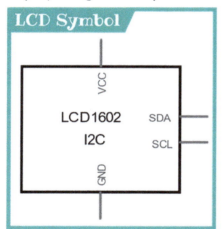

There are 4 pins on the LCD that connect to the Arduino. Two are Vcc and GND which connect to 5V and ground. The other two are used to send information to the LCD through a communication protocol called I2C ("I squared C"). The two pins used for I2C communication are called SCL (Serial CLock) and SDA (Serial DAta). This book won't go into the specifics of how this protocol works, but basically the SDA and SCL lines send and receive signals to communicate between the LCD and the Arduino which is how you will tell the LCD what to display.

The good thing is that there is already a library that makes it easy to use the LCD. It is called LiquidCrystal I2C (written by Frank de Brabander) and needs to be installed to your computer using the Arduino library manager. The specifics of how to use this library will be discussed as you go through the activities.

Activity 1 - Hello World

Overview

For this activity, you will be setting up and using the LCD to display "Hello World."

Schematic

The schematic for this circuit makes it a bit hard to see where to connect your wires, but here it is. The breadboard image below gives a better idea of the connections as the SDA and SCL pins on the board are not as obvious.

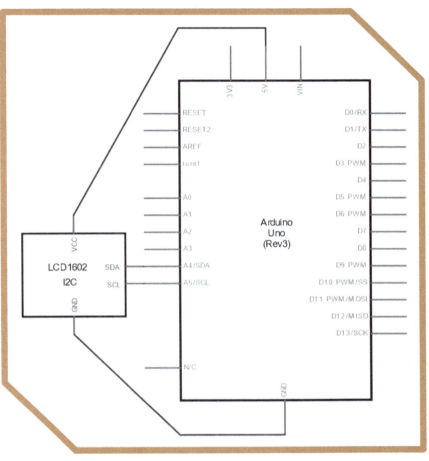

Breadboard

Below is the breadboard image. The SDA and SCL pins on the Uno board are the left two unmarked pins on the top of the board. (The pins on your board may have some kind of indication which is which.) The leftmost is SCL and the next one is SDA. VCC connects to 5V and GND connects to ground.

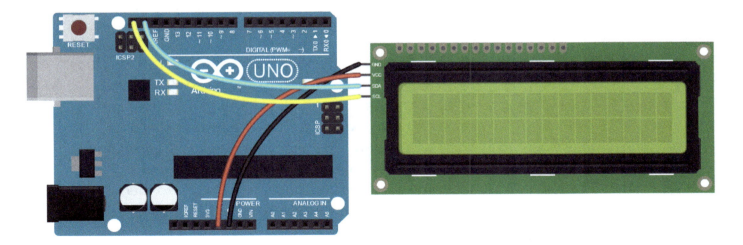

Code

Since the display only needs to be changed once, the majority of the code is in the setup function and there is nothing in the loop function. The code will be broken down line by line, but for now, here is the entirety of the code:

```cpp
#include <LiquidCrystal_I2C.h>

LiquidCrystal_I2C lcd(0x27, 16, 2);

void setup(){
  lcd.init();
  lcd.backlight();
  lcd.setCursor(0, 0);
  lcd.print("Hello World");
}

void loop(){

}
```

```cpp
#include <LiquidCrystal_I2C.h>
```
The first line tells the compiler to include the library file for the display. The directive #include is used to tell the compiler to include any files outside of the main sketch file. The # symbol identifies what is called a "directive" which is something that gives instruction to the compiler to be dealt with before compilation. The file being included with the #include directive gets enclosed in angle brackets – < > The library you are using is called "LiquidCrystal_I2C" and the .h file extension stands for header which is a type of C++ file that contains class and function declarations.

```cpp
LiquidCrystal_I2C lcd(0x27, 16, 2);
```
The next line creates an "instance" of the LiquidCrystal_I2C "class." While we will not be diving too deep into classes, you need to know how to use one. A class defines an "object," almost like a new type. A class has its own variables and functions that are used to interact with declared instances of that class. As an example, if we had a "polygon" class, we could define instances "triangle," "square," and "rectangle." Each would have the same variables and functions available to them, but the individual values of those variables would be different for each specific shape.

This specific line of code declares an instance of the LiquidCrystal_I2C class with an instance named lcd (the name could be anything as long as it follows variable naming rules). Each class also will have a specific set of variables that must be declared to initialize the instance. This will be included in parentheses after the name.

This class needs three variables to create a new instance – the address, the number of columns, and the number of rows. The address is generally pre-defined and will often be the value 0x27. This is a hexadecimal value (base 16) and is equivalent to decimal (base 10) number 39. The LCD you use has 16 columns and 2 rows.

`lcd.init();` The first line within the setup function calls the init method on the lcd. (The functions in a class are called methods and are called by naming the class instance, putting a period, the name of the method, and then in parentheses any arguments needed for that method.) This method sets up the connection to send data to the lcd and is necessary to use it. There are no arguments for this method.

`lcd.backlight();` The backlight method also does not need any arguments. This method turns on the screen backlight which is helpful in seeing the display more easily.

`lcd.setCursor(0, 0);` Next is the setCursor method. This method will tell the LCD where the cursor goes. It has two arguments, column and row numbers. This will set the location to display information The columns and rows of the LCD are indexed in the same way as an array, starting at 0. Column values would be 0–15 and row values would be 0–1. In this activity you will begin displaying in the top left corner, so column 0, row 0.

`lcd.print("Hello World");` Lastly, print to the display using the print method. This works like the Serial monitor print function (because Serial is a class instance!). Therefore, you can print any value such as a variable, function return value, or just a string. The print method will only print on the row where the cursor is, so if the input is too long to fit on the row, it will only print the characters that fit and any others will not be displayed. To print on a different row, the cursor needs to be moved. In this case, you are printing the string "Hello World".

Activity 2 - Stopwatch

Overview

In this activity, you will be building a simple stopwatch. It will have two buttons: start/stop and reset. The start/stop button will start the stopwatch (when it was previously stopped) or start the stopwatch (when it was previously running). If the stopwatch is stopped, the reset button will reset the time back to zero.

Schematic

The circuit for this activity adds two buttons to the LCD circuit from the last assignment. Each will get connected with a pull-down resistor to a digital pin (pins 2 and 3).

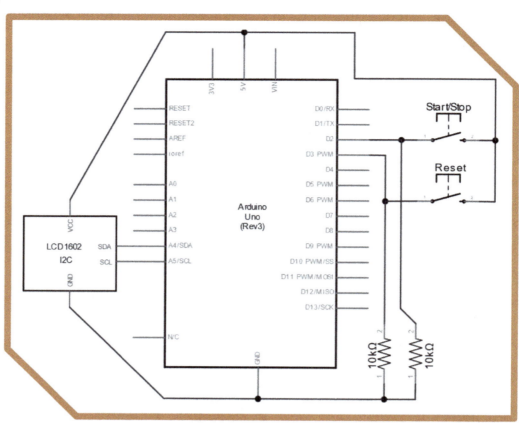

Breadboard

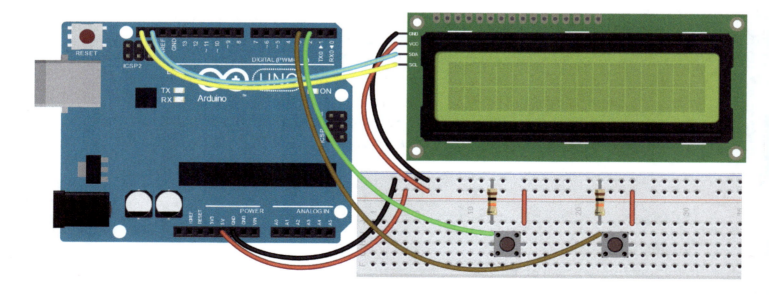

Code

For this assignment, some of the code is provided. The rest will be left for you to fill in, following along with pseudocode comments.

Here is all of the code before the setup function and the pseudocode for the setup function:

Loop Function

The general idea of the loop part of the program is as follows: You will check the start/stop button. If the button gets pressed, the stopwatch will start or stop based on whether it was running or not before the button press. To run the stopwatch, you will use the millis() built-in function. This function returns the number of milliseconds the program has been running. Doing some math, you can determine how long the stopwatch has been running and output that to the lcd. When the reset button is pressed, the time resets to 0.

```cpp
#include <LiquidCrystal_I2C.h>

//pins
int ssButton = 2;
int resetButton = 3;

//pin readings
int ssButtonVal;
int startVal;

//flags
bool running = false;
bool reset = true;

LiquidCrystal_I2C lcd(0x27, 16, 2);
void setup()
{
  //initialize button pins to input

  //initialize the lcd
  //turn on the backlight

  //set cursor to column 0, row 0
  //print "Time: 00:00.000" on lcd

  //set cursor to column 0, row 1
  //print "Start/Stop Reset" on lcd
}
```

As an outline: The first while loop starts the stopwatch as long as the button is pressed and the stopwatch is not yet running. The second while loop makes sure the button press is finished before starting the stopwatch. The third while loop stops the stopwatch as long as the button is pressed and the stopwatch is already running. The fourth while loop makes sure the button press is finished before stopping the stopwatch. And, the if statement resets the time if the reset button is pressed.

There is also a new function you will see below: sprintf. This is a C language function that allows you to easily format data for printing – it saves the results to a character array, which is why the array timeDisp is created. That way the time will be formatted as 00:00.00 with minutes, seconds, and milliseconds.

```
void loop()
{
  ssButtonVal = digitalRead(ssButton);

  while(ssButtonVal == HIGH and running == false){
    ssButtonVal = digitalRead(ssButton);
    startVal = millis();

    if(reset == false){startVal = millis()-currVal;}

    while(ssButtonVal == LOW){
      //set reset flag to false (time is no longer 0 and thus not reset)
      //set running flag to true (stopwatch is now running)

      // calculate the current time value by finding current millis and
                subtracting the start time
      // calculate minutes (integer) by dividing the current time value by
                60000
      // calculate seconds (integer) by dividing the current value by 1000
      // calculate milliseconds by finding the remainder of dividing the
                current time value by 1000 (modulus)

      char timeDisp[9];
      sprintf(timeDisp, "%02d:%02d.%03d",minutes,seconds,millisecs);

      //set lcd cursor to column 6, row 0
      //print timeDisp array to lcd

      ssButtonVal = digitalRead(ssButton);
    }
  }

  while(ssButtonVal == HIGH and running == true){
    ssButtonVal = digitalRead(ssButton);

    while(ssButtonVal == LOW){
      //set running flag to false (stopwatch is no longer running)

      if(digitalRead(resetButton) == HIGH and reset == false){
        //set reset flag to true (time has been reset to 0)
        //set cursor to column 0, row 0
        //print "Time: 00:00.000" on lcd
      }

      ssButtonVal = digitalRead(ssButton);
    }
  }
}
```

Conclusion

In this lesson, you used a new component: the LCD, which uses a communication protocol called I2C. You also used our first library: LiquidCrystal I2C.

In the next lesson you will be using another new component and associated library.

Lesson 11 - Typing Stuff
Using a Keypad

In this lesson, you will be using a new component, the keypad (specifically one called a membrane keypad). It is an input component that allows you to submit button presses to the Arduino. It is arranged in a grid of 16 buttons – 4 buttons by

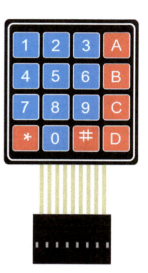

buttons. This includes the digits 0–9, the letters A–D, the pound character (#), and the asterisk character (*). It connects to the Arduino using 8 digital pins.

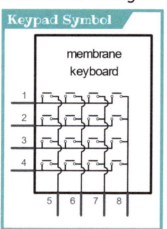

The membrane keypad is a "button matrix." Buttons are connected to the Arduino in rows and columns. All the buttons are normally open. When one is pressed, it closes that row and column. The Arduino is used to determine which row and column have a closed button, and thus which button is pressed.

This can be seen in the schematic view of the keypad. As an example, if you close the third button on the second row, that change can be seen in the third column, second row.

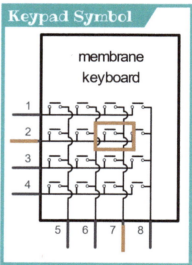

Using a Keypad - Coding the Membrane Keypad

To use a keypad, you will be using the Keypad library by Mark Stanley and Alexander Brevig. This allows you to connect the keypad directly to the Arduino and easily read button presses.

Keypad Initialization

```
#include <Keypad.h>
```

Use the #include directive to include the keypad library header file in your code. The file is Keypad.h. So, at the top of your file you would have the line

To set up a keypad in your code, you need to create an object, or "class instance" of the Keypad class. You can define a new keypad by using the type Keypad, choosing a name for your keypad (can be any valid variable name) and setting that equal to the Keypad "constructor" (the initialization function for the class. This declaration takes 5 arguments which will be discussed individually.

```
Keypad keypad = Keypad( makeKeymap(keys), rowPins, colPins, ROWS, COLS );
```

```
char keys[ROWS][COLS] = {
  {'1','2','3','A'},
  {'4','5','6','B'},
  {'7','8','9','C'},
  {'#','0','*','D'}
};
```

The first argument is a call to the macro makeKeymap() which is part of the Keypad library. (A macro is a short piece of code that gets defined to get replaced by a certain value.) makeKeymap() takes one argument, keys, which is a two dimensional array (basically an array where the array elements are arrays) of the type char. This array tells the Arduino what character each key represents. The size of the array is based on two variables: ROWS and COLS which hold the size of the keypad.

```
byte rowPins[ROWS] = {9,8,7,6};
byte colPins[COLS] = {5,4,3,2};
```

The next two arguments are the arrays rowPins and colPins which are both the type byte. They contain the pins that are connected to the keypad.

```
const byte ROWS = 4;
const byte COLS = 4;
```

The last two arguments of the keypad initialization are ROWS and COLS which hold the number of rows and number of columns of the keypad, respectively. These have the type byte. The keyword const tells the Arduino that the variable is a constant and thus cannot be changed.

Here is the complete initialization code for the keypad:

```
#include <Keypad.h>
const byte ROWS = 4;
const byte COLS = 4;
char keys[ROWS][COLS] = {
  {'1','2','3','A'},
  {'4','5','6','B'},
  {'7','8','9','C'},
  {'#','0','*','D'}
};

byte rowPins[ROWS] = {9,8,7,6};
byte colPins[COLS] = {5,4,3,2};

Keypad keypad = Keypad( makeKeymap(keys), rowPins, colPins, ROWS, COLS );
```

Getting a Key Press

```
char key = keypad.getKey();
```

To read a key press, you will use the getKey() method. This method returns a char so a variable needs to be created to hold this value. To determine if a key has been pressed, you can compare the key press to the variable NO_KEY.

Activity - Reading Keys

Overview

This activity will allow you to try using a keypad for input. You will be using two devices: a keypad and a seven-segment display. The keypad will be used to enter key presses and the seven-segment display will display those key presses.

Schematic

For this circuit, the keypad connects to pins 2–9. The seven-segment display connects to pins 10–13 on top. On the bottom, since there are no more digital pins available, you will use analog pins A3–A5 for the remaining pins. They can be used just like digital pins, setting them up with the pinMode function.

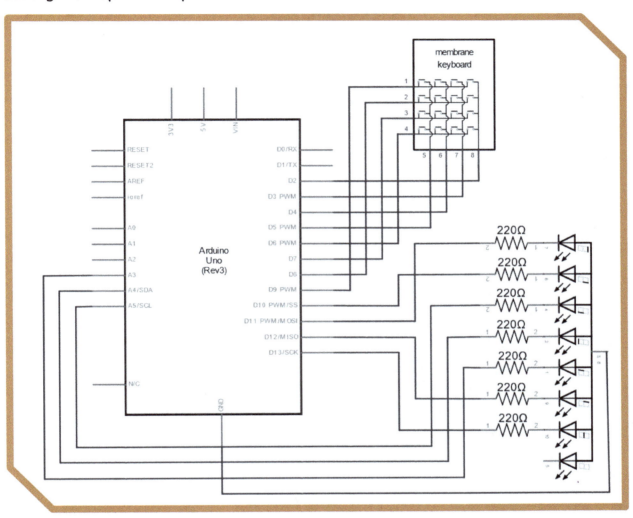

Breadboard

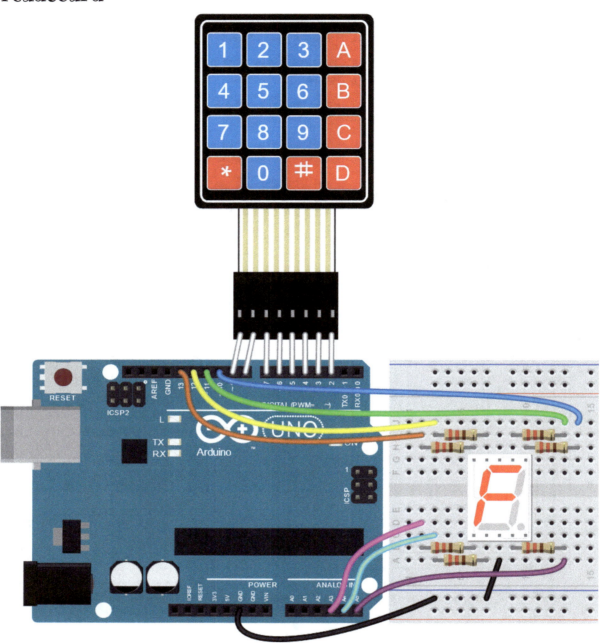

Code

Before the setup function, you need to declare an array to hold the pins for the seven-segment display. You also need to declare the arrays to display each value on the seven-segment display. (It has been left up to you to determine what to display for the pound and asterisk characters.) Also before the setup function, is the initialization code for the keypad. (Make sure to have #include <Keypad.h> at the top of your code as well.)

```cpp
#include <Keypad.h>
int sevSeg[] = {13,12,11,10,A3,A4,A5};

int one[]   = {0,0,0,1,0,0,1};
int two[]   = {1,0,1,1,1,1,0};
int three[] = {1,0,1,1,0,1,1};
int four[]  = {1,1,0,1,0,0,1};
int five[]  = {1,1,1,0,0,1,1};
int six[]   = {1,1,1,0,1,1,1};
int seven[] = {0,0,1,1,0,0,1};
int eight[] = {1,1,1,1,1,1,1};
int nine[]  = {1,1,1,1,0,0,1};
int zero[]  = {0,1,1,1,1,1,1};
int a[]     = {1,1,1,1,1,0,1};
int b[]     = {1,1,0,0,1,1,1};
int c[]     = {0,1,1,0,1,1,0};
int d[]     = {1,0,0,1,1,1,1};
int pound[] = {???};
int ast[]   = {???};
const byte ROWS = 4;
const byte COLS = 4;
char keys[ROWS][COLS] = {
  {'1','2','3','A'},
  {'4','5','6','B'},
  {'7','8','9','C'},
  {'#','0','*','D'}
};

byte rowPins[ROWS] = {9,8,7,6};
byte colPins[COLS] = {5,4,3,2};

Keypad keypad = Keypad( makeKeymap(keys), rowPins, colPins, ROWS, COLS );
```

In the setup function, you need to set up the pins of the seven-segment display for output. You can use a for loop to loop through the array that contains the pin numbers. You do not need to set up the pins of the keypad as the class takes care of this for you.

```
void setup(){
   for(int i=0; i < 8; i++){
      pinMode(sevSeg[i],OUTPUT);
   }
}
```

The loop function begins with checking for a key press. The if statement following checks to see if the key press has a value. If it does, you need to display that value on the seven-segment display. We can do this using a switch statement. Each character on the keypad will have a separate case. Each case will have a for loop that loops through the pin numbers of the seven-segment display and sends high/low signals based on the corresponding array for that character.

Here is the first part of the loop function. This includes the first case of the switch statement. You will need to complete the other cases, changing the character and corresponding array for each.

```
void loop(){
   char key = keypad.getKey();

   if (key != NO_KEY){
      switch(key){
         case '1':
            for(int i = 0; i < 8; i++){
               digitalWrite(sevSeg[i],one[i]);
            }
            break;
         . . .
```

Conclusion

In this lesson, you used a new component, the membrane keypad and its corresponding library, the Keypad library.

In the next lesson, you will be putting together the concepts learned in the last two lessons in a review project.

Lesson 12 - Keeping Score
Making a Digital Scoreboard

Activity - Scoreboard

Overview

In this lesson, you are going to be reviewing topics that have been covered in previous lessons by making a simple digital scoreboard. Two scores will be displayed on an LCD. Scores will be entered with a keypad. Here is an example of what will be displayed on the LCD:

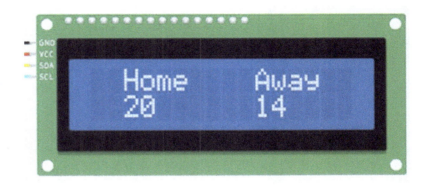

Here is the basic functionality of the keypad:

- The A and B buttons will be used to set the score for either home or away, respectively.
- Once the score to set (home/away) has been selected:
  - Enter a score using the numerical digits.
  - Finalize the score with the # key.
  - Additionally, the * key can be used to set the score to 0.

Schematic

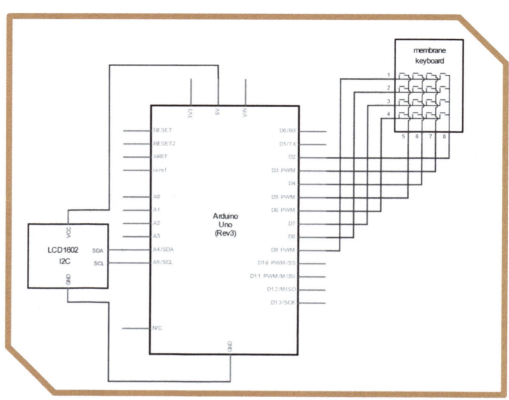

Breadboard

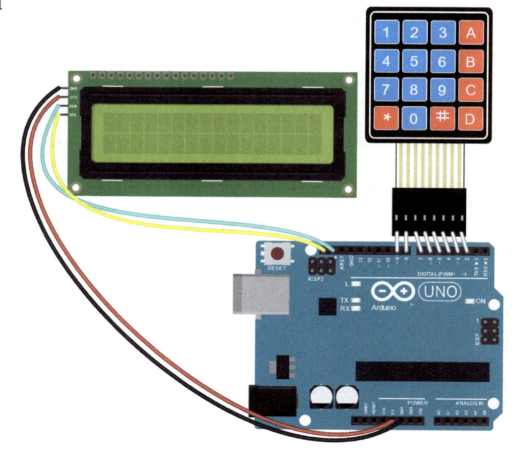

Code

Before the setup function, you need to initialize the LCD and keypad by creating a class instance of each. This includes creating each of the variables for the keypad initialization function.

```cpp
#include <Keypad.h>
#include <LiquidCrystal_I2C.h>
LiquidCrystal_I2C lcd(0x27, 16, 2);

const byte ROWS = 4; //four rows
const byte COLS = 4; //four columns
char keys[ROWS][COLS] = {
  {'1','2','3','A'},
  {'4','5','6','B'},
  {'7','8','9','C'},
  {'*','0','#','D'}
};
byte rowPins[ROWS] = {9,8,7,6};
byte colPins[COLS] = {5,4,3,2};
Keypad keypad = Keypad( makeKeymap(keys), rowPins, colPins, ROWS, COLS );
```

```cpp
int colPos = 0;
```

You also need to create an integer variable to hold the column position for displaying the scores. It will be used in the loop function. For now, set it to 0.

In the setup function, you need to initialize the LCD and turn on the backlight. Additionally, display the Home/Away heading on the top row of the LCD – this won't change throughout the program so it just needs to be set once.

```cpp
void setup() {
  lcd.init(); //initialize the lcd
  lcd.backlight(); //turn on the backlight

  lcd.setCursor(0, 0);
  lcd.print("  Home    Away");
}
```

In the loop function, first read the keypad to get the score to set. This is saved as the char variable teamKey. The if statement that follows will determine if a key has been pressed. The rest of the code will be inside this if statement.

```
void loop() {
  char teamKey = keypad.getKey();

  if (teamKey != NO_KEY){
```

```
if(key == 'A'){ colPos = 2; }
else if(teamKey == 'B'){ colPos = 10; }
```

The next if and else if statement will set the column position based on which team is selected. The home score will be column 2 and the away score will be column 10.

```
lcd.setCursor(colPos, 1);
lcd.print("          ");
lcd.setCursor(colPos, 1);
lcd.blink();
```

Next, clear the current score by printing over it with spaces. Then, we will set the cursor back to the start of the score position to be entered. The blink method blinks the cursor to make it obvious when a score is being entered.

```
char scoreKey = keypad.getKey();

while(scoreKey != '#' and scoreKey != '*'){
  if(scoreKey != NO_KEY){ lcd.print(scoreKey); }
  scoreKey = keypad.getKey();
}
```

Then, the score can be entered, one digit at a time, each getting stored in the variable scoreKey. The while loop that follows will allow the Arduino to keep accepting digits for the score as long as the key entered is not a # or a *.

Inside the while loop, the lcd will print each key press and then check for another key press.

```
char scoreKey = keypad.getKey();

while(scoreKey != '#' and scoreKey != '*'){
  if(scoreKey != NO_KEY){ lcd.print(scoreKey); }
  scoreKey = keypad.getKey();
}
```

Note 1: the if statement is necessary to make sure only actual key press values are printed.

Note 2: The while loop will continue running until a # or * is read from the keypad. So, there is technically no way to prevent a score being entered that is either long enough to overwrite the other score or overflow off the edge of the screen.

Conclusion

In this lesson we reviewed previous concepts, including using the LCD and keypad and their respective classes by building a digital scoreboard.

While this project could be greatly expanded on with additional programming and features, hopefully this gives you a basic idea of a real-world project that can be easily built with an Arduino.

Lesson 13 - Motors Part 1
DC Motors

Spin Spin Spin - Introduction to Motors

Types of Motors

There are three types of motors commonly used with Arduinos which will be discussed in the next few lessons:

- DC Motors
- Servo Motors
- Stepper Motors

Each type works a bit differently and has different applications.

DC Motors

A DC motor uses direct current electricity to convert electricity into mechanical force. Generally this is accomplished through a magnet and coil system. DC motors spin in a single direction. They turn on and begin spinning as soon as power is applied.

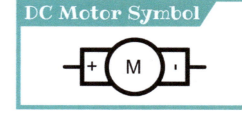

DC Motor Symbol

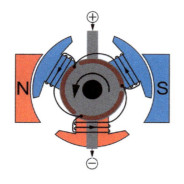

A DC Motor consists of coils of wire attached to a rotating center axle. On the outside, there are permanent magnets. The coils are energized by a power source in order to attract/repel the magnets to rotate the axle.

Making Things Spin - Using DC Motors

New Component - Transistor

gate   source
drain

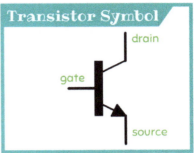

Transistor Symbol

drain

gate

source

You are going to be using a new component called a transistor to help control our motor. Specifically, you will be using what's called an n-channel MOSFET. Transistors have three pins - called the gate, drain, and source.

Transistors can work a bit like a control valve. In this lesson you will use them to send a signal from the Arduino through the gate which tells how much flow should go between the drain and source - kind of like a handle on a faucet. This allows you to use a low current device (Arduino) to control a device that requires a high current (motor).

New Component - Diode

A diode is a component that allows current to only flow in a single direction. You have already used LEDs which are light-emitting diodes, so diodes that emit light when current passes through them. In this lesson, you will use a diode to prevent backflow current which can sometimes happen when turning off a DC motor.

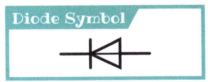

Diode Symbol

DC Motor Circuit

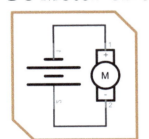

Let's build a DC motor circuit one component at a time. The most basic way to run a DC motor is to put a battery on it. Note: Polarity is not all that important with DC motors - changing the polarity will simply change the direction of rotation.

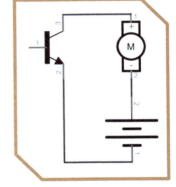

Next, in order to control the motor with an Arduino, we need to add in a transistor. The drain of the transistor will connect to one side of the motor. The source will connect to the negative side of the battery. This will create a loop with the battery, motor, and transistor.

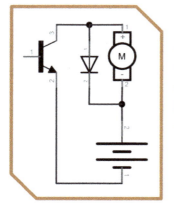

Additionally, we will add a diode in parallel to the motor. When motors turn off, they can create a large voltage spike which could potentially damage other circuit components. The diode helps to dissipate this safely and prevent current from flowing the wrong direction through the circuit.

Lastly, we can connect the Arduino to this circuit. Digital pin 9 connects to the gate of the transistor. We will use a PWM signal to control the motor. Also, we need to create a "common ground" for our circuit by connecting the ground pin to the negative side of the battery. This connects all the grounds together and helps the circuit to function properly.

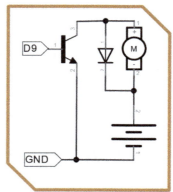

Here is an example of what a DC motor circuit might look like on a breadboard. The battery used in this example is a 9V battery with clip. A separate battery/power source must be used to power a DC motor as the Arduino does not provide enough current to power one.

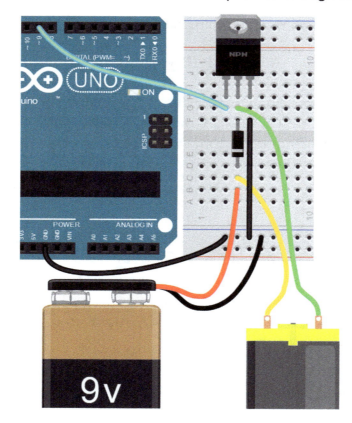

Activity 1 - Changing Speeds

Overview

In this assignment, you will be controlling the speed of a dc motor with a potentiometer. You can use PWM and the map function to convert the potentiometer reading to a value that can be sent to the motor.

Schematic

For this circuit, you will use a DC motor circuit connected to pin 9 and a potentiometer circuit connected to pin A0. The battery used is a 9V battery with a clip that can be plugged into a breadboard.

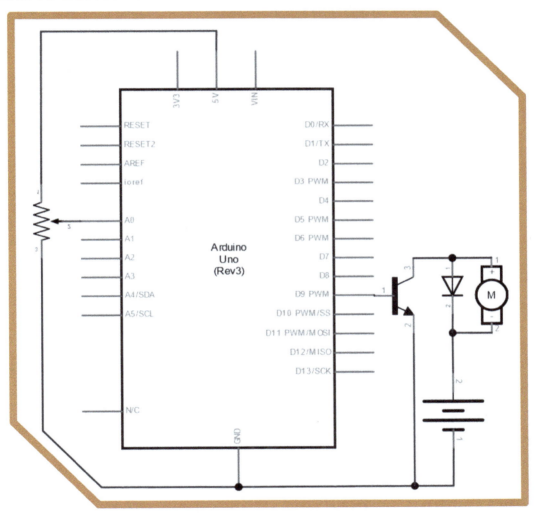

Breadboard

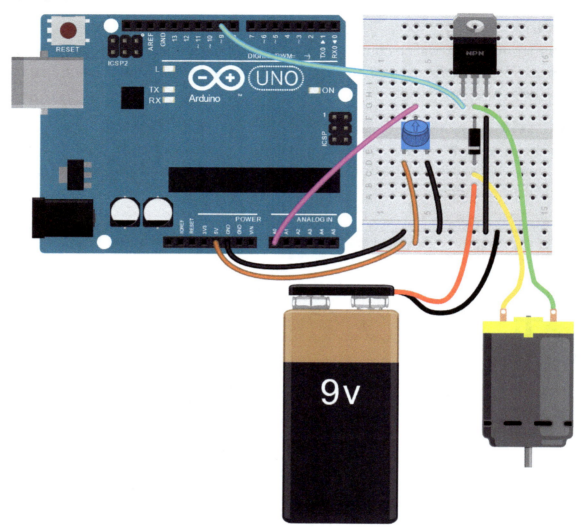

Code

Since all of the code in this project has been covered before and the program is very short, below is a very basic outline of the pseudocode to write your code from.

- Set the motor pin to output
- Read the value of the potentiometer
- Convert this value to a PWM usable value with the map function
- Output the mapped value to the motor pin using PWM

(If you want a challenge, the loop function could be written in a single line.)

Conclusion

In this lesson, you learned about DC motors – how they work and how to use them. The speed of DC motors can be controlled using a transistor circuit and a PWM signal from the Arduino.

In the next lessons you will be learning about two other types of motors – servo and stepper motors.

Lesson 14 - Motors Part 2
Servo Motors

In the Last Lesson...

In the last lesson it was mentioned that there are three main types of motors that you will be using:

- DC Motors
- Servo Motors
- Stepper Motors

You learned about and used DC motors. Let's briefly review how a DC motor works. A DC motor uses direct current electricity to convert electricity into mechanical force. Generally this is accomplished through a magnet and coil system. A DC Motor consists of coils of wire attached to a rotating center axle. On the outside, there are permanent magnets. The coils are energized by a power source in order to attract/repel the magnets to rotate the axle.

Controlled Spinning - Servo Motors

In this lesson, you will be working with servo motors. Servo motors are motors that contain a feedback system. They allow a signal to set the motor to a certain position. The motor will stay in that position until a new position signal is sent. A servo motor consists of a DC motor, gear assembly, potentiometer, and controlling circuit. Servos can typically move over a range of 180 degrees. A servo has 3 pins – power (red), ground (black), and a control signal (yellow). The control signal can connect to any PWM pin of the Arduino.

To use a servo with an Arduino, install the Servo library by Michael Margolis and Arduino. This introduces a Servo class that allows you to easily control servo motors. You will go through the specifics of how to use the class in activity 1.

Activity 1 - Point the Way

Overview

In this assignment, the goal is to learn how to use a servo and corresponding Arduino library. You will be using two buttons to adjust the servo left or right. The servo will rotate while a button is pressed and stop when no buttons are pressed.

Schematic

Here is the schematic for the circuit. The servo connects to power, ground, and pin 9. Two buttons are connected to pins 2 and 3 along with pull-down resistors.

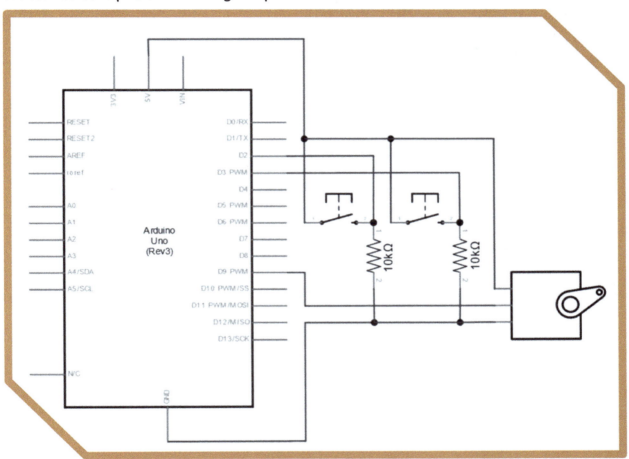

Breadboard

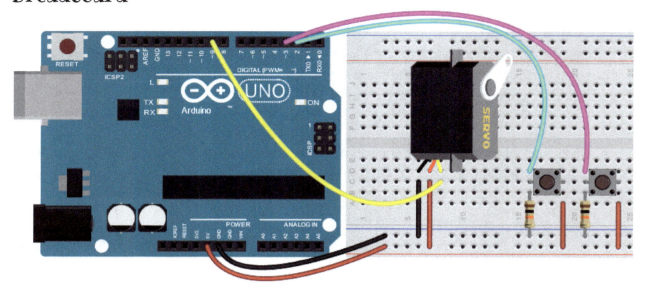

Code

```
#include <Servo.h>
Servo myServo;
int servoPos = 0;
```

The code for this assignment will be looked at line–by–line so you can see how to program a servo. First, include the header file Servo.h. Next, create a new Servo object. Here it is named myServo. There aren't any required arguments for the constructor. These lines go before the setup function. The only other thing before the setup function is an integer variable called servoPos which will be set equal to 0. This will indicate the position of the servo and will be used in the loop function.

```
void setup() {
  myServo.attach(9);
  myServo.write(servoPos);

  pinMode(2,INPUT);
  pinMode(3, INPUT);
}
```

In the setup function, initialize the servo, starting with the method attach. This has a single integer argument which is the pin connected to the servo. Then use the write method to position the servo to 0 (servoPos variable). The write method can take argument values 0–180, representing degree measurements. Also in the setup function, use the pinMode function to initialize the two buttons to input.

```
void loop() {
  while(digitalRead(2) == HIGH and servoPos > 0){
  }
  while(digitalRead(3) == HIGH and servoPos < 180){
  }
}
```

The loop function has two while loops – one for each button. The left button will decrease the servo position and the right button will increase the servo position. The first while loop will check to see if pin 2 is high (left button pressed) and the servo position is greater than 0. The second while loop will check to see if pin 3 is high (right button pressed) and the servo position is less than 180. The while loops each have a conditional statement to prevent the program from setting a higher/lower value than the servo will allow.

Inside the first while loop, you will decrement the servo position using the decrement operator. Then write the new position to the servo. You will do the same thing in the other while loop but with the increment operator.

```
void loop() {
  while(digitalRead(2) == HIGH and servoPos > 0){
    servoPos--;
    myServo.write(servoPos);
  }
  while(digitalRead(3) == HIGH and servoPos < 180){
    servoPos++;
    myServo.write(servoPos);
  }
}
```

Activity 2 - Garage Door Opener

Overview

In this activity, you will be using a servo and button to simulate a garage door. The servo will move back and forth along its rotation to simulate the door opening. When the button is pressed, the door will either open or close (depending on previous open/closed state).

Schematic

This circuit is the same as activity 1 but with only one button (pin 2).

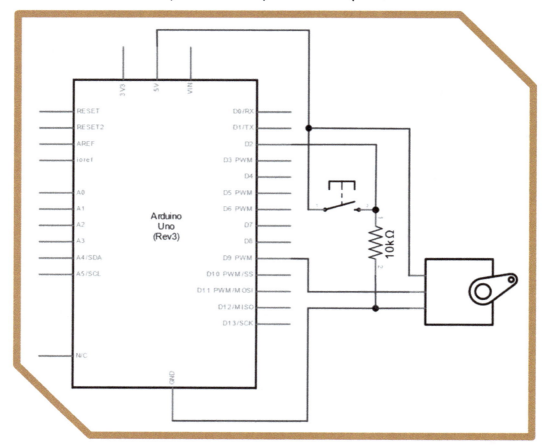

Breadboard

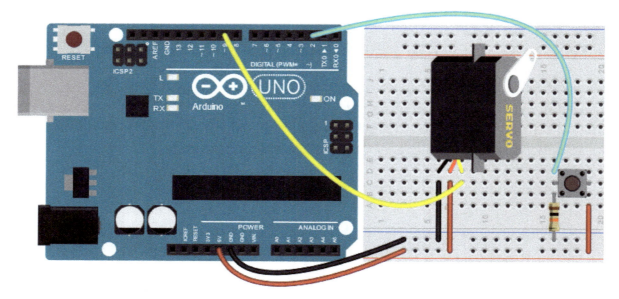

Code

The servo setup code remains much the same as activity 1. Before the setup function you need two flag variables – one to indicate position (open or closed) and one to indicate a new button press. The setup function will initialize the servo and button. The pseudocode for the entire program is below.

```
•  Before setup:
    •  Include servo header and initialize new servo.
    •  Set position flag (posFlag) variable to 0
    •  Set new button press flag(newFlag) variable to 1
•  Setup function:
    •  Attach servo to pin 9 and write the value 0 to it.
    •  Set the button (pin 2) to input.
•  Loop function:
    •  Set newFlag to 1 (new button press)
    •  Read the button pin
    •  While the button is pressed:
        •  If the posFlag is 1 and newFlag is 1 (servo is in
           position 1 and there is a new button press):
            •  Set the servo to 0 degrees
            •  Set posFlag and newFlag to 0 (servo is now
               in position 0 and there is no new button
               press)
        •  If the posFlag is 0 and newFlag is 1 (servo is in
           position 0 and there is a new button press):
            •  Set the servo to 180 degrees
            •  Set posFlag to 1 and newFlag to 0 (servo is
               now in position 1 and there is no new button
               press)
    •  Read the button pin
```

Conclusion

In this lesson, you learned about servo motors. Servo motors are DC motors with feedback and the ability to set a position.

In the next lesson the discussion of motors will be continued in learning about stepper motors.

Lesson 15 - Motors Part 3
Motors Review (So Far)

In this lesson, you will be putting together the first two motor lessons in a review assignment. You will have a new sensor component to use along with a DC motor and Servo motor.

How Hot Is It? - Using a Temperature Sensor

First up, let's introduce a new component – a temperature sensor (specifically the TMP36). This is an analog sensor that changes value based on the temperature it reads. It has a reading range of –40 degrees C to 150 degrees C (–40 degrees F to 302 degrees F) and outputs a voltage in the range of 0.1 V to 2.0 V which can be read by an analog pin of the Arduino. (Note: some sensors may have a limit of 125 degrees C and 1.75 V.)

The temperature and voltage form a linear relationship which makes it simple to calculate the temperature from the voltage of the sensor.

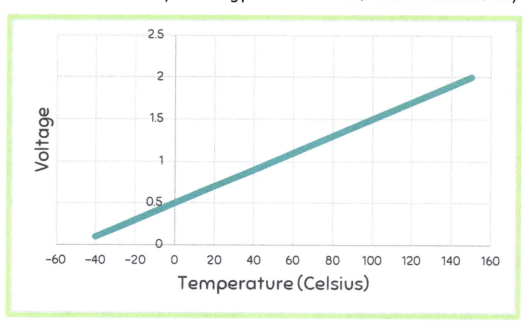

To calculate the temperature from a sensor reading, we must first calculate the voltage being outputted by the sensor:

$$voltage = sensorValue \times \frac{5}{1024}$$

The ADC converts 5 volts into 1024 steps. By dividing 5 by 1024 we can figure out how much voltage each step represents. We can then figure out the voltage of the sensor reading by multiplying the voltage of 1 step by how many steps in the sensor value. Note: the sensorValue comes from performing an analogRead on the analog pin in which the sensor is attached.

Next, we can use the voltage to calculate the temperature in Celsius:

$$Celsius = (voltage - 0.5) \times 100$$

We first subtract 0.5 from the voltage because the TMP36 has a 0.5 V offset to allow for negative temperature readings. This value gets multiplied by 100 because the sensor has a scaling factor of 10 mV/degree C.

Next, we can use the voltage to calculate the temperature in Celsius:

$$Celsius = (voltage - 0.5) \times 100$$

We first subtract 0.5 from the voltage because the TMP36 has a 0.5 V offset to allow for negative temperature readings. This value gets multiplied by 100 because the sensor has a scaling factor of 10 mV/degree C.

Finally, we can calculate the temperature in Fahrenheit:

$$Fahrenheit = \left(Celsius \times \frac{9}{5}\right) + 32$$

This equation is the Celsius to Fahrenheit conversion formula.

Here is the set of equations written in code, beginning with a read of the sensor. Notice that the equations all use the

```
int sensorVal = analogRead(A0);
float voltage = sensorVal * (5.0 / 1024.0);
float tempC = (voltage - 0.5) * 100;
float tempF = (tempC * 9.0 / 5.0) + 32.0;
```

variable type float. This allows the equations to produce decimal answers. Decimals are also used for all the values in the equations to ensure that float values are produced correctly.

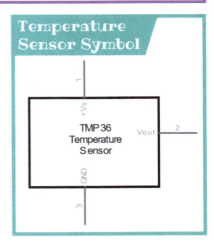

Temperature Sensor Symbol

The TMP36 has 3 pins, Vs, Vout, and GND. On the Arduino, Vs connects to 5V, Vout connects to an analog pin, and GND connects to GND. Once connected, the sensor can be read using the analogRead function. That value can then be used to calculate the temperature.

Activity - Temperature Controlled Fan

Overview

In this assignment, you will be combining the temperature sensor along with motor circuits you have previously built to create a temperature controlled fan. A DC motor will act as the fan and using PWM, you can map values from the temperature sensor to the motor to adjust the speed. A servo motor will act as a gauge to show how hot/cold the temperature is.

Schematic

This circuit has three main sections:

- The servo motor
- The DC motor
- The temperature sensor

Note: Using the servo library causes the PWM on pins 9 and 10 to not work so make sure you don't use one of these for the DC motor.

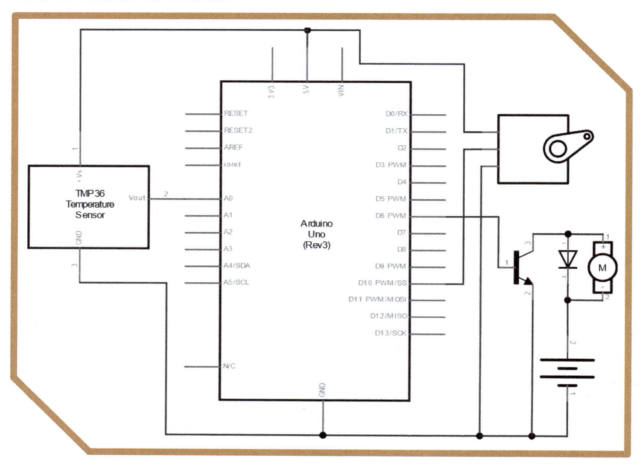

Breadboard

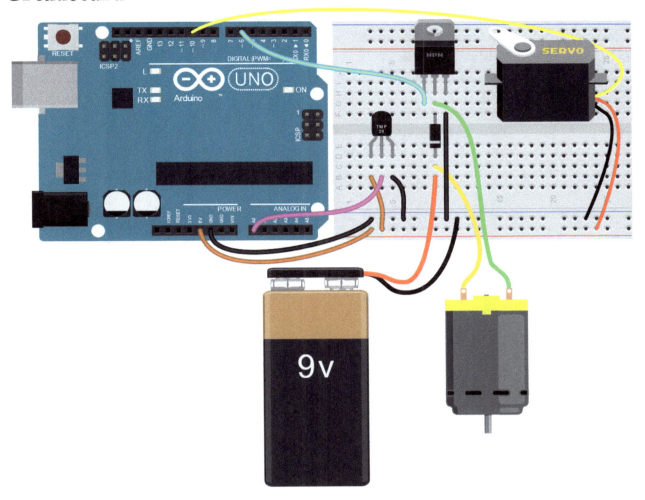

Code

Below is a general overview of the code. You may want to go back and reference the initialization code for DC and Servo motors. from the last two lessons. You may also find it helpful to use the serial monitor as you test your code.

```
• Initialize a servo and attach it to pin 10.
• The DC motor will be on pin 6.
• Inside the loop function:
    • Read the sensor (pin A0) - This value needs to be saved
      as a variable.
    • Perform calculations to find Fahrenheit value.
    • Use an if/else if/else statement to set speed of motor
      and servo position. Below are the ranges and values.
        • Temp > 100: Set DC motor to 30 and servo to 144
        • Temp > 74: Set DC motor to 25 and servo to 108
        • Temp > 50: Set DC motor to 20 and servo to 72
        • Otherwise (Temp <= 50): Set DC motor to 0 and servo
          to 36
    • Delay the program by 1 second. (This helps reduce
      electrical noise in the servo.)
```

Conclusion

In this lesson you reviewed what has been covered so far involving motors – using a DC and servo motor. You also used a new component – the TMP36 temperature sensor.

In the next lesson, you will conclude your study of motors by learning about stepper motors.

Lesson 16 - Motors Part 4
Stepper Motors

Introduction - Refreshing Some Topics

In this lesson you will be revisiting a couple components from earlier lessons. Since it's been a little while since you used them, let's take a moment to review.

The RGB LED you use is a common cathode. The "common" pin (which is the longest) connects to ground. The other three pins each connect to a digital pin (generally a PWM pin), including a current-limiting resistor for each pin as well. In this lesson you will just be using HIGH/LOW values so you won't be using PWM.

Also, as a reminder the piezo buzzer connects to a digital pin. It uses the tone function to play a tone (at a given frequency) and the noTone function to turn off the tone.

Specific Spinning - Stepper Motors

Stepper motors work very much the same as a DC motor, but with many more "steps." (A DC motor might have 3 steps, whereas a stepper motor often has around 200, or even 2000, depending on the gearing of the specific motor.) Using the Stepper library you can tell the Arduino exactly how many steps to move the motor – and thus how far you want it to spin.

You are using the 28BYJ–48 stepper motor and ULN2003 control board. The stepper connects to the board via a plug that plugs directly into the board. The board connects to the Arduino on pins 8, 9, 10, and 11 (IN1, IN2, IN3, and IN4, respectively). The Arduino does not have enough power supply to turn on the stepper, however so an external power supply is needed – you will use a battery. The positive side of the battery will connect to the + pin and the – pin will connect to the negative side of the battery and ground of the Arduino.

Here is how the stepper motor and board will appear in schematic drawings:

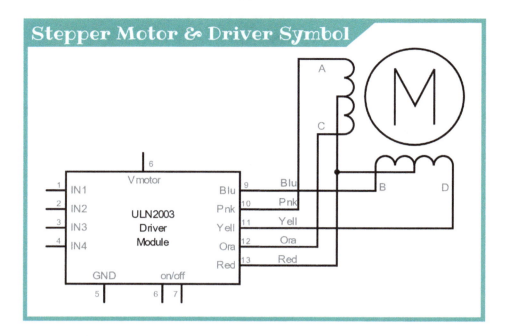

To program a stepper motor, you will be using the Stepper library by Arduino. To initialize a stepper, call the name of the library, name the motor, and then include necessary arguments. The first argument is the number of steps per revolution. In this case, 2048. The next 4 arguments are the connected pins. Assuming pin 8 is connected to IN1, pin 9 is connected to IN2, etc., the order of the pins in the arguments is 8, 10, 9, 11. This order has to do with the order of how the pins are used on the motor.

There are two methods you will be using from the Stepper library.

```
Stepper myStepper(2048, 8, 10, 9, 11);
```

The first is setSpeed. This allows you to set the speed of the stepper in rotations per minute (rpms). Note that this does not move the stepper, but just sets the speed for when you do tell it to move.

```
myStepper.setSpeed(rpm);
```

The second method you will use is the step method. This tells the motor how many steps to move. For this motor, a full rotation is 2048 steps.

```
myStepper.step(steps);
```

Activity 1 - Stepper Motor Timer

Overview

In this assignment, you are building a one-minute timer using a stepper motor, RGB LED, button, and piezo. A button will be used to start the timer. Once started, the stepper motor will rotate once around at a speed of 1 rpm. The RGB LED will display a blue light when the timer is not running, a green light during the first 45 seconds of the timer, a yellow light (red and green) during the next 10 seconds, and a red light during the last 5 seconds. A piezo will play a tone for 3 seconds at the end of the timer.

Schematic

The circuit for this activity has four main components – the RGB LED (with current-limiting resistors), a button (with a pull-down resistor), a piezo buzzer, and the stepper motor/control board.

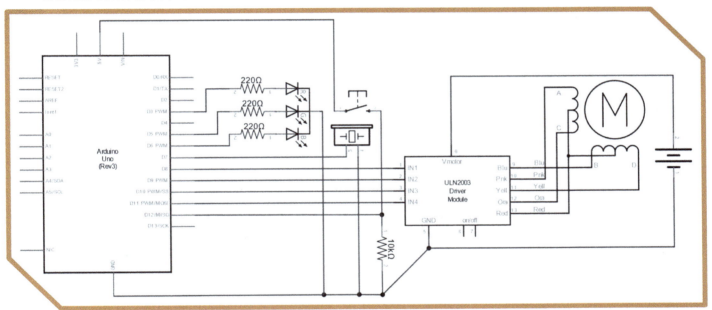

Breadboard

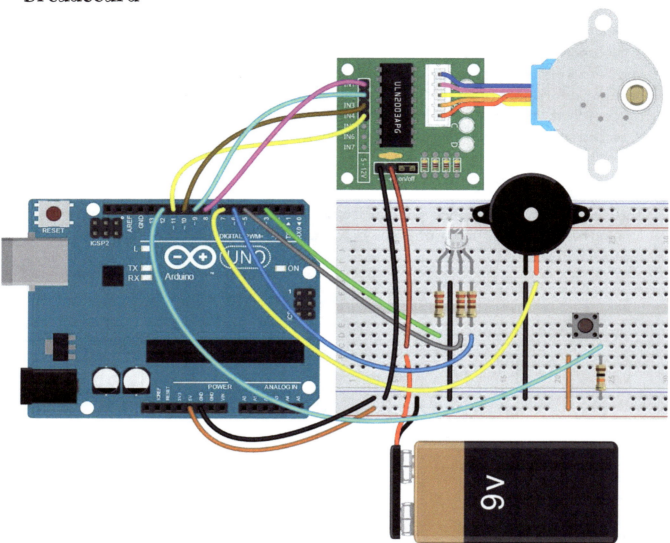

Calculations

Before getting into the code, let's do a couple calculations. Since the LED needs to change colors during the rotation of the motor, we need to split the motor rotation into pieces to change turn on/off LED pins between the pieces. For the first 45 seconds, the light will be green. We know the motor goes through 2048 steps in one revolution. So, we can use a proportion of 2048 steps and 60 seconds to figure out how many steps are in 45 seconds.

Calculating steps for 45 seconds:

$$\frac{2048\ steps}{60\ seconds} = \frac{x\ steps}{45\ seconds}$$

$$x \, steps = 45 \, seconds \times \frac{2048 \, steps}{60 \, seconds} = 1536 \, steps$$

For the next 10 seconds of the timer, the LED is yellow. Calculating the number of steps in 10 seconds:

$$\frac{2048 \text{ steps}}{60 \text{ seconds}} = \frac{x \text{ steps}}{10 \text{ seconds}}$$

$$x \text{ steps} = 10 \text{ seconds} \times \frac{2048 \text{ steps}}{60 \text{ seconds}} = 341.333 \text{ steps} \approx 341 \text{ steps}$$

For the final 5 seconds of the timer, the LED is red. Calculating the number of steps in 5 seconds:

$$\frac{2048 \text{ steps}}{60 \text{ seconds}} = \frac{x \text{ steps}}{5 \text{ seconds}}$$

$$x \text{ steps} = 5 \text{ seconds} \times \frac{2048 \text{ steps}}{60 \text{ seconds}} = 170.667 \text{ steps} \approx 171 \text{ steps}$$

Code Outline

- Before setup function:
    - Include and initialize stepper library/motor using 2048 steps per revolution and pins 8, 10, 9, and 11.
    - Make variables for all other pin numbers (since there are so many pins being used, this will make the rest of the program much easier to write).
- Setup function:
    - Initialize all pins (other than stepper motor pins) to INPUT/OUTPUT.
    - Turn off red and green lights and turn on blue light.
- Loop function:
    - If the button is pressed (start the timer):
        - Turn blue light off and green light on.
        - Set speed of motor to 1 rpm.
        - Step motor first interval (45 seconds) and then turn on red light (red and green light combined make yellow).
        - Step motor second interval (10 seconds) and then turn off green light.
        - Step motor third interval and then turn off red light.
        - Play a tone on the buzzer for 3 seconds.
    - After the if statement, turn the blue light back on.

Conclusion

In this lesson, you finished up the study of motors with learning about stepper motors. Stepper motors allow you to precisely control the speed and position of the motor shaft.

This is the last lesson of this book! Hopefully at this point you have learned the basics of using a variety of components with the Arduino and you can utilize these skills in the development of your own creative projects.

References

Musical Note Frequencies

Octave	Note	Frequency
0	B	31
1	C	33
	C# (Db)	35
	D	37
	D# (Eb)	39
	E	41
	F	44
	F# (Gb)	46
	G	49
	G# (Ab)	52
	A	55
	A# (Bb)	58
	B	62
2	C	65
	C# (Db)	69
	D	73
	D# (Eb)	78
	E	82
	F	87
	F# (Gb)	93
	G	98
	G# (Ab)	104
	A	110
	A# (Bb)	117
	B	123
3	C	131
	C# (Db)	139
	D	147
	D# (Eb)	156
	E	165
	F	175
	F# (Gb)	185
	G	196
	G# (Ab)	208
	A	220
	A# (Bb)	233
	B	247

Octave	Note	Frequency
4	C	262
	C# (Db)	277
	D	294
	D# (Eb)	311
	E	330
	F	349
	F# (Gb)	370
	G	392
	G# (Ab)	415
	A	440
	A# (Bb)	466
	B	494
5	C	523
	C# (Db)	554
	D	587
	D# (Eb)	622
	E	659
	F	698
	F# (Gb)	740
	G	784
	G# (Ab)	831
	A	880
	A# (Bb)	932
	B	988
6	C	1047
	C# (Db)	1109
	D	1175
	D# (Eb)	1245
	E	1319
	F	1397
	F# (Gb)	1480
	G	1568
	G# (Ab)	1661
	A	1760
	A# (Bb)	1865
	B	1976

Octave	Note	Frequency
7	C	2093
	C# (Db)	2217
	D	2349
	D# (Eb)	2489
	E	2637
	F	2794
	F# (Gb)	2960
	G	3136
	G# (Ab)	3322
	A	3520
	A# (Bb)	3729
	B	3951
8	C	4186
	C# (Db)	4435
	D	4699
	D# (Eb)	4978

Major Scales

Scale	Notes							
C	C	D	E	F	G	A	B	C
G	G	A	B	C	D	E	F#	G
D	D	E	F#	G	A	B	C#	D
A	A	B	C#	D	E	F#	G#	A
E	E	F#	G#	A	B	C#	D#	E
B	B	C#	D#	E	F#	G#	A#	B
F#	F#	G#	A#	B	C#	D#	E# (F)	F#
Gb	Gb	Ab	Bb	Cb (B)	Db	Eb	F	Gb
Db	Db	Eb	F	Gb	Ab	Bb	C	Db
C#	C#	D#	E# (F)	F#	G#	A#	B# (C)	C#
Ab	Ab	Bb	C	Db	Eb	F	G	Ab
Eb	Eb	F	G	Ab	Bb	C	D	Eb
Bb	Bb	C	D	Eb	F	G	A	Bb
F	F	G	A	Bb	C	D	E	F

Programming Reference Sheet

Note: this reference sheet is not exhaustive of all Arduino functionality but it contains all/most of the functionality you will need in this book.

Data Types
int
bool
float
long
byte
void

Digital Functions

```
pinMode(pinNum, INPUT/OUTPUT)
digitalRead(pinNum)
digitalWrite(pinNum, HIGH/LOW)
```

Analog Functions

```
analogRead(pinNum)
analogWrite(pwmPinNum, value)
```

Declaring a variable

```
type variableName = value;
```

Declaring an array

```
type arrayName[] = {val1, val2, val3};
```

Built-in Functions

map(value, fromLow, fromHigh, toLow, toHigh)	delay(millisecs)
delayMicroseconds(microsecs)	Millis()
tone(pinNum, frequency)	random(endVal)
tone(pinNum, frequency, duration)	random(startVal, endVal)
noTone(pinNum)	pulseIn(pinNum, value)

Mathematical Operators

Addition	+
Subtraction	−
Division	/
Multiplication	*
Remainder	%
Assignment	=

Conditional Operators

equal to	==
less than	<
less than or equal to	<=
greater than	>
greater than or equal to	>=
not equal to	!=

Logical Operators

and	&&
or	||
not	!

Compound Operators

Increment	++
Decrement	--
Compound Addition	+=
Compound Subtration	-=

Conditional Statements

```
if(condition1){
   //if condition1 is true,
this code executes
}
else if(condition2){
   //if condition2 is true,
this code executes
}
else{
   //if all conditions are
false, this code executes
}
```

```
switch(variableName){
   case 1:
      //if variableName == val1
      break;
   case val2:
      //if variableName == val2
      break;
   default:
      //if variableName is not equal to any
case value
}
```

Loops

```
while(condition){
   //while condition is true,
this code executes
}
```

```
for(startVal; condition; increment){
   //beginning with startVal,
   //code executes while condition is true
}
```

Serial Monitor

begin()
print(printVal)
println(printVal)

Keypad Library

Keypad keypadName(makeKeymap(keys), rowPins,colPins, ROWS, COLS)
getKey()

Stepper Library

Stepper stepperName(numOfSteps, pinNum1, pinNum2)
setSpeed(rpms)
step(numOfSteps)

Liquid Crystal I2C Library

LiquidCrystal_I2C lcdName(address, columns, rows)
init()
backlight()
setCursor(col, row)
print(printVal)

Servo Library

Servo servoName
attach(pinNum)
write(angle)
read()
attached()
detached()

Arduino Component List

Input Components

- **Push Button**
  - Schematic

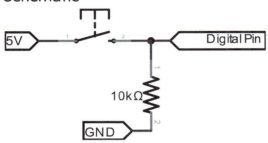

  - Breadboard

  - Description
    - Connects (with a pull-down resistor) to a single digital pin. Pin reads HIGH when button is pressed and LOW when button is not pressed.

- **Switch (1 pin)**
  - Schematic

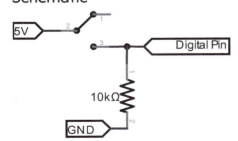

○ Breadboard

○ Description
- Connects (with a pull-down resistor) to a single digital pin. Pin reads HIGH when switch is switched toward pin connection and LOW when switch is switched away from pin connection.

- Switch (2 pin)
  ○ Schematic

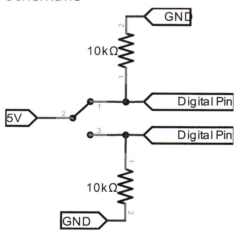

  ○ Breadboard

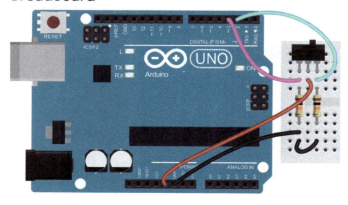

- o Description
  - Connects (with pull-down resistors) to two digital pins – one on each side of the switch and ground in the middle. A pin reads HIGH when switch is switched toward that pin connection and LOW when switch is switched away from that pin connection.

- **Potentiometer**
  - o Schematic

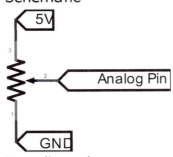

  - o Breadboard

  - o Description
    - Connects to power, ground, and an analog pin. Acts as a variable resistor voltage divider. The pin will read analog values converted to digital values 0–1023, depending on the position of rotation.

- Keypad
  - Schematic

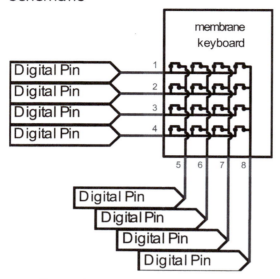

  - Breadboard

- Description
  - Use along with the Keypad library. Connects to 8 digital pins. Library converts button presses to character values.

- Photoresistor
  - Schematic

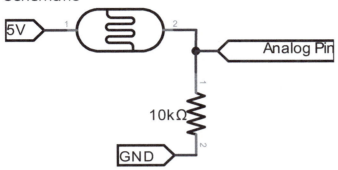

  - Breadboard

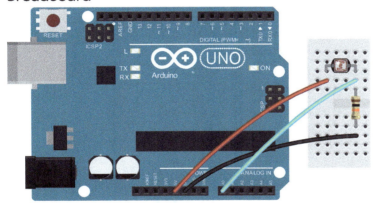

  - Description
    - Acts as a variable resistor. Wired as a voltage divider with an analog pin. Pin reads analog values converted to digital 0–1023, depending on light levels. Resistor value may need to be adjusted depending on ambient light levels.

- Tilt Switch
  - Schematic

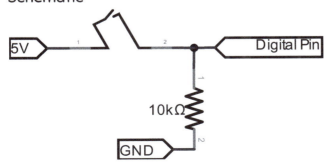

o Breadboard

o Description
▪ Connects (with a pull-down resistor) to a single digital pin. Pin reads HIGH when switch is upright and LOW when switch is tilted.

- **Ultrasonic Sensor**
  o Schematic

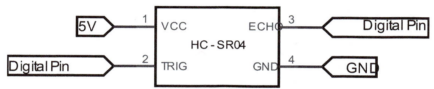

  o Breadboard

  o Description
  ▪ Connects to two digital pins, power, and ground. Use to measure an object's distance from sensor. Trig pin sends a ping and echo pin measures the time it takes for the ping to return to the sensor.

- **Temperature Sensor**
  - Schematic

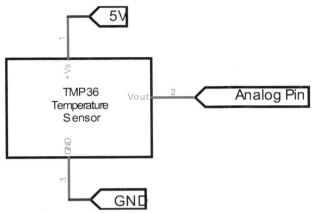

  - Breadboard

  - Description
    - Measures temperature and reports it as a voltage. Temperature can be calculated from analog pin readings.

Output Components

- **LED**
  - Schematic

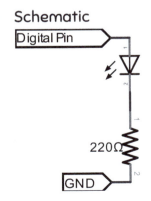

- Breadboard

- Description
  - Connects to a digital pin and ground (along with a current-limiting resistor). Emits light when HIGH signal sent and turns off when LOW signal sent.

- **RGB LED**
  - Schematic

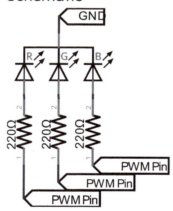

  - Breadboard

- o Description
  - ▪ Connects to 3 PWM pins (with current-limiting resistors) and ground. Each pin controls a separate color – red, green, and blue. PWM values 0–255 will adjust the brightness of each color.

- Seven-Segment Display
  - o Schematic

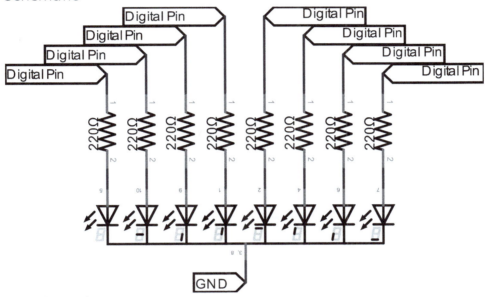

  - o Breadboard

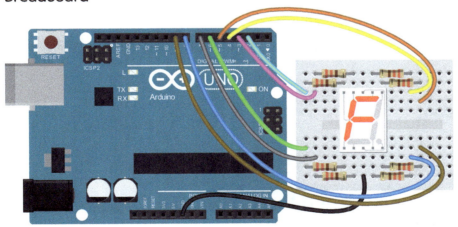

  - o Description
    - ▪ Connects to 8 digital pins along with current-limiting resistors. Can display numerals and other characters by writing high/low values to each pin.

- LCD
  - Schematic

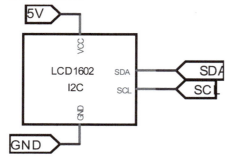

  - Breadboard

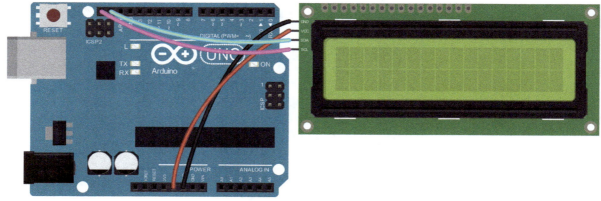

  - Description
    - Uses I2C communication and the LiquidCrystal_I2C library. Can display 2 rows of 16 characters (including custom characters).

- Buzzer
  - Schematic

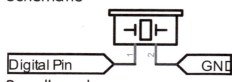

  - Breadboard

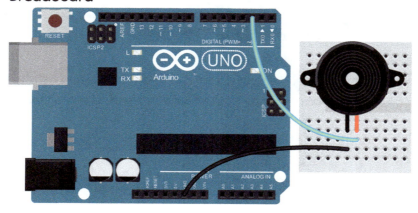

- Description
    - Connects to a digital pin and ground. Plays a sound using the tone and noTone functions at given frequencies.

- DC Motor
    - Schematic

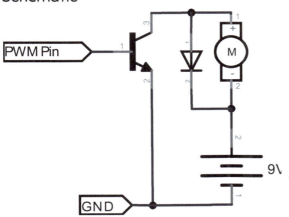

    - Breadboard

    - Description
        - Connects to a PWM pin. Speed can be adjusted using different PWM values. Must be connected to an external power source.

- **Servo Motor**
  - Schematic

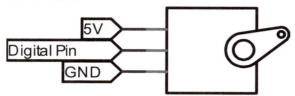

  - Breadboard

  - Description
    - Uses the Servo library. Connects to power, ground, and a digital pin. Set position by writing a degree value to the motor.

- **Stepper Motor**
  - Schematic

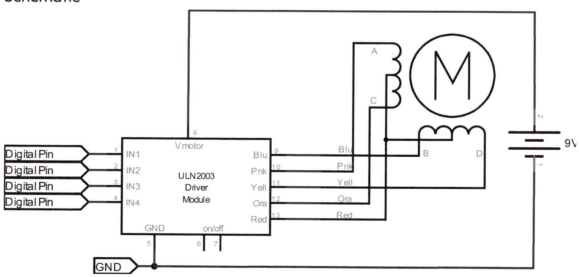

o Breadboard

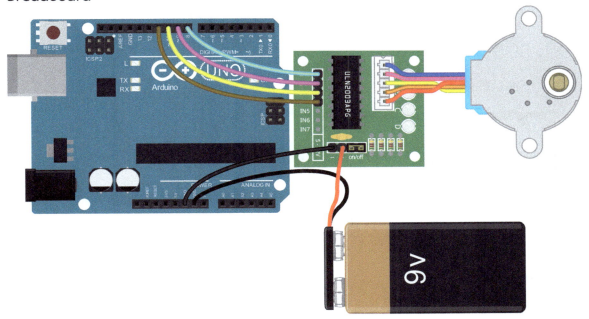

o Description
  ▪ Uses the Stepper library. Set speed of rotation and number of steps to move. Connects to 4 digital pins (8, 9, 10, 11). Must be connected to an external power source.

Solutions

Download all code files at: https://github.com/janna-camp/Arduino-Made-Easy

Lesson 1

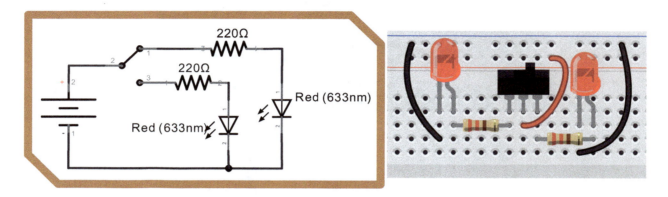

Lesson 2

Activity 1 – Blinky Blinky

```
void setup() {
  pinMode(2,OUTPUT); //LED pin
}

void loop() {
  digitalWrite(2,HIGH); //Turn LED on
  delay(1000); //Wait 1 second
  digitalWrite(2,LOW); //Turn LED off
  delay(1000); //Wait 1 second
}
```

Lesson 3

Activity 1 – One-Way Traffic Signal

```
int green = 2; //Schematic: LED3
int yellow = 3; //Schematic: LED2
int red = 4; //Schematic: LED1

void setup() {
  //Initialize LED pins to output
  pinMode(green, OUTPUT);
  pinMode(yellow, OUTPUT);
  pinMode(red, OUTPUT);

  //Turn green and yellow off and red on
  digitalWrite(green, LOW);
  digitalWrite(yellow, LOW);
```

```
    digitalWrite(red, HIGH);
}

void loop() {
  delay(5000); //5 seconds for red light

  //Turn red off and green on
  digitalWrite(red, LOW);
  digitalWrite(green, HIGH);
  delay(5000); //5 seconds for green light

  //Turn green off and yellow on
  digitalWrite(green, LOW);
  digitalWrite(yellow, HIGH);
  delay(2000); //2 seconds for yellow light

  //Turn yellow off and red on
  digitalWrite(yellow, LOW);
  digitalWrite(red, HIGH);
}
```

Activity 2 – Four-Way Traffic Signal

```
int red_1 = 4; //Schematic: LED4
int yellow_1 = 3; //Schematic: LED5
int green_1 = 2; //Schematic: LED6

int red_2 = 7; //Schematic: LED10
int yellow_2 = 6; //Schematic: LED11
int green_2 = 5; //Schematic: LED12

int red_3 = 8; //Schematic: LED9
int yellow_3 = 9; //Schematic: LED8
int green_3 = 10; //Schematic: LED7

int red_4 = 11; //Schematic: LED3
int yellow_4 = 12; //Schematic: LED2
int green_4 = 13; //Schematic: LED1

// Pairs of Lights: 1/4 ; 2/3

void setup() {

  //Set all LED pins to output
  pinMode(green_1, OUTPUT);
  pinMode(yellow_1, OUTPUT);
  pinMode(red_1, OUTPUT);
```

```
  pinMode(green_2, OUTPUT);
  pinMode(yellow_2, OUTPUT);
  pinMode(red_2, OUTPUT);

  pinMode(green_3, OUTPUT);
  pinMode(yellow_3, OUTPUT);
  pinMode(red_3, OUTPUT);

  pinMode(green_4, OUTPUT);
  pinMode(yellow_4, OUTPUT);
  pinMode(red_4, OUTPUT);

  ///////////////////////////////////

  //Turn all red lights on and all green and yellow lights off
  digitalWrite(green_1, LOW);
  digitalWrite(yellow_1, LOW);
  digitalWrite(red_1, HIGH);

  digitalWrite(green_2, LOW);
  digitalWrite(yellow_2, LOW);
  digitalWrite(red_2, HIGH);

  digitalWrite(green_3, LOW);
  digitalWrite(yellow_3, LOW);
  digitalWrite(red_3, HIGH);

  digitalWrite(green_4, LOW);
  digitalWrite(yellow_4, LOW);
  digitalWrite(red_4, HIGH);
}

void loop() {

  delay(1000); //1 second of all red lights

  ///////////////////////////////////

  //Turn 2 & 3 red off and green on
  digitalWrite(red_2, LOW);
  digitalWrite(red_3, LOW);
  digitalWrite(green_2, HIGH);
  digitalWrite(green_3, HIGH);

  delay(5000); //5 seconds of 2 & 3 green
```

```
//Turn 2 & 3 green off and yellow on
digitalWrite(green_2, LOW);
digitalWrite(green_3, LOW);
digitalWrite(yellow_2, HIGH);
digitalWrite(yellow_3, HIGH);

delay(2000); //2 seconds of 2 & 3 yellow

///////////////////////////////////////

//Turn 2 & 3 yellow off and red on
digitalWrite(yellow_2, LOW);
digitalWrite(yellow_3, LOW);
digitalWrite(red_2, HIGH);
digitalWrite(red_3, HIGH);

delay(1000); //1 second of all red

///////////////////////////////////////

//Turn 1 & 4 red off and green on
digitalWrite(red_1, LOW);
digitalWrite(red_4, LOW);
digitalWrite(green_1, HIGH);
digitalWrite(green_4, HIGH);

delay(5000); //5 seconds of 1 & 4 green

//Turn 1 & 4 green off and yellow on
digitalWrite(green_1, LOW);
digitalWrite(green_4, LOW);
digitalWrite(yellow_1, HIGH);
digitalWrite(yellow_4, HIGH);

delay(2000); //2 seconds of 1 & 4 yellow

///////////////////////////////////////

//Turn 1 & 4 yellow off and red on
digitalWrite(yellow_1, LOW);
digitalWrite(yellow_4, LOW);
digitalWrite(red_1, HIGH);
digitalWrite(red_4, HIGH);
}
```

Lesson 4

Activity 1 – Button Pushing

```
void setup() {
  pinMode(2, OUTPUT); //LED set to output
  pinMode(3, INPUT); //button set to input
}

void loop() {
  if(digitalRead(3) == HIGH){ //if button is pressed
    digitalWrite(2, HIGH); //turn LED on
  }
  else{ //if button is not pressed
    digitalWrite(2, LOW); //turn LED off
  }
}
```

Activity 2 – Button Buzzer

```
void setup() {
  pinMode(2, INPUT); //button set to input
  pinMode(3, OUTPUT); //buzzer set to output
}

void loop() {
  if(digitalRead(2) == HIGH){ //if button is pressed
    tone(3, 440); //play note
  }
  else{ //if button is not pressed
    noTone(3); //stop note
  }
}
```

Lesson 5

Activity 1 – Mini Piano

```
int buzzer = 10; //buzzer pin

//note frequencies
int c1 = 262;
int d = 294;
int e = 330;
int f = 349;
int g = 392;
int a = 440;
int b = 494;
int c2 = 523;

void setup() {
  //for loop to set pins 2-9 to input (buttons)
  for(int i = 2; i < 10; i++){
```

```
      pinMode(i,INPUT);
  }
  pinMode(buzzer, OUTPUT); //set buzzer pin to output
}

void loop() {
  //read each button press
  int button1 = digitalRead(2);
  int button2 = digitalRead(3);
  int button3 = digitalRead(4);
  int button4 = digitalRead(5);
  int button5 = digitalRead(6);
  int button6 = digitalRead(7);
  int button7 = digitalRead(8);
  int button8 = digitalRead(9);

  //if/else if/else statement to check button values
  //if a button is high, that frequency will play
  //if multiple buttons are pressed, the first button pressed
will be the frequency played
  //if no button is pressed, buzzer will be turned off

  if(button1 == HIGH){
    tone(buzzer, c1);
  }
  else if(button2 == HIGH){
    tone(buzzer, d);
  }
  else if(button3 == HIGH){
    tone(buzzer, e);
  }
  else if(button4 == HIGH){
    tone(buzzer, f);
  }
  else if(button5 == HIGH){
    tone(buzzer, g);
  }
  else if(button6 == HIGH){
    tone(buzzer, a);
  }
  else if(button7 == HIGH){
    tone(buzzer, b);
  }
  else if(button8 == HIGH){
    tone(buzzer, c2);
  }
  else{
    noTone(buzzer);
  }
}
```

Activity 1 Project Extension

```
int buzzer = 10; //buzzer pin
int notes[] = {262, 294, 330, 349, 392, 440, 494, 523}; //note
     //frequencies
int buttons[] = {0,0,0,0,0,0,0,0}; //array to hold button pin
     //read values

void setup() {
  //for loop to set pins 2-9 to input
  for(int i = 2; i < 10; i++){
    pinMode(i,INPUT);
  }
  pinMode(buzzer, OUTPUT); //buzzer pin set to output
}

void loop() {
  //for loop uses numbers 0-7 to set button array values
  //array values are digital readings of pins 2-9
  for(int i = 0; i < 8; i++){
    buttons[i] = digitalRead(i+2);
  }

  //if/else if/else statement to check button values
  //if a button is high, that frequency will play
  //if multiple buttons are pressed, the first button pressed
  //will be the frequency played
  //if no button is pressed, buzzer will be turned off

  if(buttons[0] == HIGH){
    tone(buzzer, notes[0]);
  }
  else if(buttons[1] == HIGH){
    tone(buzzer, notes[1]);
  }
  else if(buttons[2] == HIGH){
    tone(buzzer, notes[2]);
  }
  else if(buttons[3] == HIGH){
    tone(buzzer, notes[3]);
  }
  else if(buttons[4] == HIGH){
    tone(buzzer, notes[4]);
  }
  else if(buttons[5] == HIGH){
    tone(buzzer, notes[5]);
  }
  else if(buttons[6] == HIGH){
    tone(buzzer, notes[6]);
  }
  else if(buttons[7] == HIGH){
    tone(buzzer, notes[7]);
```

```
    }
    else{
      noTone(buzzer);
    }
}
```

Lesson 6a

Activity 1 – Electronic Die #1

```
int tilt = 9; //tilt switch pin
int tiltState; //integer to hold the value of the tilt switch pin
int rolled = 0; //flag to show if die has been rolled
int off = 0; //flag to show if lights are off
int LEDs[] = {2,3,4,5,6,7,8}; //LED pins

// LED pin layout:
// 2      6
// 3   5  7
// 4      8

// arrays for displaying each number
// Pins:       2,3,4,5,6,7,8
int one[]   = {0,0,0,1,0,0,0};
int two[]   = {1,0,0,0,0,0,1};
int three[] = {1,0,0,1,0,0,1};
int four[]  = {1,0,1,0,1,0,1};
int five[]  = {1,0,1,1,1,0,1};
int six[]   = {1,1,1,0,1,1,1};

void setup() {
  //for loop to set LED pins to output (0-7 index values for LED
    //array)
  for(int i = 0; i < 8; i++){
    pinMode(LEDs[i], OUTPUT);
  }

  pinMode(tilt, INPUT); //set tilt switch pin to input

  //for loop to turn all LEDs off
  for(int i = 0; i < 8; i++){
    digitalWrite(LEDs[i], LOW);
  }
}

void loop() {
  tiltState = digitalRead(tilt); //read tilt switch

  while(tiltState == LOW){ //while tilt switch is tilted (die is
          //being rolled)
    if(off == 0){ //if LEDs are not off, turn them all off and
          //set off flag to 1
```

```
      for(int i = 0; i < 7; i++){
        digitalWrite(LEDs[i],LOW);
      }
      off = 1;
    }

    tiltState = digitalRead(tilt); //read tilt switch
    rolled = 1; //die has been rolled
}

//if switch is not tilted (die is not being rolled) and die has
        //been rolled (rolled flag)
if(tiltState == HIGH and rolled == 1){
    rolled = 0; //reset rolled flag as roll will be fulfilled
            //once if statement completes
    off = 0; //reset off flag as LEDs will be on once if
            //statement completes
    int dice = random(1,7); //create variable to hold roll value
            //- random value 1-6

    switch(dice){ //switch statement contains cases for each
            //possible die value each case has a for loop that
            //sets each LED to 0/1 based on corresponding die
            //value array

      case 1:
        for(int i = 0; i < 7; i++){
          digitalWrite(LEDs[i],one[i]);
        }
        break;
      case 2:
        for(int i = 0; i < 7; i++){
          digitalWrite(LEDs[i],two[i]);
        }
        break;
      case 3:
        for(int i = 0; i < 7; i++){
          digitalWrite(LEDs[i],three[i]);
        }
        break;
      case 4:
        for(int i = 0; i < 7; i++){
          digitalWrite(LEDs[i],four[i]);
        }
        break;
      case 5:
        for(int i = 0; i < 7; i++){
          digitalWrite(LEDs[i],five[i]);
        }
        break;
      case 6:
        for(int i = 0; i < 7; i++){
```

```
            digitalWrite(LEDs[i],six[i]);
        }
        break;
      }
    }
  }
```

Lesson 6b

Activity 2 – Electronic Die #2

```
int tilt = 9; //tilt switch pin
int tiltState; //integer to hold the value of the tilt switch pin
int rolled = 0; //flag to show if die has been rolled
int off = 0; //flag to show if lights are off
int sevSeg[] = {2,3,4,5,6,7,8}; //seven segment display pins

// arrays for displaying each number
// Pins:        2,3,4,5,6,7,8
int one[]   = {0,0,0,1,0,0,1};
int two[]   = {1,0,1,1,1,1,0};
int three[] = {1,0,1,1,0,1,1};
int four[]  = {1,1,0,1,0,0,1};
int five[]  = {1,1,1,0,0,1,1};
int six[]   = {1,1,1,0,1,1,1};

void setup() {
  //for loop to set seven segment pins to output
  for(int i = 2; i < 9; i++){
    pinMode(i, OUTPUT);
  }
  pinMode(tilt, INPUT); //set tilt switch pin to input

  //for loop to turn all LEDs off
  for(int i = 0; i < 8; i++){
    digitalWrite(sevSeg[i], LOW);
  }
}

void loop() {
  tiltState = digitalRead(tilt); //read tilt switch

  while(tiltState == LOW){ //while tilt switch is tilted (die is
         //being rolled)
    if(off == 0){ //if LEDs are not off, turn them all off and
         //set off flag to 1
      for(int i = 0; i < 8; i++){
        digitalWrite(sevSeg[i],LOW);
      }
      off = 1;
    }
```

```
      tiltState = digitalRead(tilt); //read tilt switch
      rolled = 1; //die has been rolled
  }

  //if switch is not tilted (die is not being rolled) and die has
          //been rolled (rolled flag)
  if(tiltState == HIGH and rolled == 1){
    rolled = 0; //reset rolled flag as roll will be fulfilled
            //once if statement completes
    off = 0; //reset off flag as LEDs will be on once if
            //statement completes
    int dice = random(1,7); //create variable to hold roll value
            //- random value 1-6

    switch(dice){ //switch statement contains cases for each
            //possible die value each case has a for loop that
            //sets each segment to 0/1 based on corresponding
            //die value array

      case 1:
        for(int i = 0; i < 8; i++){
          digitalWrite(sevSeg[i],one[i]);
        }
        break;
      case 2:
        for(int i = 0; i < 8; i++){
          digitalWrite(sevSeg[i],two[i]);
        }
        break;
      case 3:
        for(int i = 0; i < 8; i++){
          digitalWrite(sevSeg[i],three[i]);
        }
        break;
      case 4:
        for(int i = 0; i < 8; i++){
          digitalWrite(sevSeg[i],four[i]);
        }
        break;
      case 5:
        for(int i = 0; i < 8; i++){
          digitalWrite(sevSeg[i],five[i]);
        }
        break;
      case 6:
        for(int i = 0; i < 8; i++){
          digitalWrite(sevSeg[i],six[i]);
        }
        break;
    }
  }
}
```

Lesson 7

Activity 1 – Buzzing About

```
//buzzer: pin 2
//potentiometer: pin A0

void setup() {
  pinMode(2,OUTPUT); //set buzzer pin to output
}

void loop() {
  //map value of potentiometer from analog range 0-1023 to
  //frequency range 31-5000
  int freqVal = map(analogRead(A0),0,1023,31,5000);
  tone(2,freqVal); //play mapped frequency on buzzer
}
```

Activity 2 – Color Adjusting (Version 1)

```
//pin numbers for RGB LED pins
int red = 9;
int green = 10;
int blue = 11;

//pin numbers for potentiometer pins
int redPot = A0;
int greenPot = A1;
int bluePot = A2;

void setup() {
  //set LED pins to output
  pinMode(red,OUTPUT);
  pinMode(green,OUTPUT);
  pinMode(blue,OUTPUT);
}

void loop() {
  // map each potentiometer value from analog range 0-1023 to PWM
  //range 0-255
  int redVal   = map(analogRead(redPot),0,1023,0,255);
  int greenVal = map(analogRead(greenPot),0,1023,0,255);
  int blueVal  = map(analogRead(bluePot),0,1023,0,255);

  //write each mapped value to LED pins
  analogWrite(red,redVal);
  analogWrite(green,greenVal);
  analogWrite(blue,blueVal);
}
```

Activity 2 – Color Adjusting (Version 2)

```
void setup() {
  //set LED pins to output
```

```
    pinMode(9,OUTPUT);
    pinMode(10,OUTPUT);
    pinMode(11,OUTPUT);
}

void loop() {
    // map each potentiometer value from analog range 0-1023 to PWM
    //range 0-255 and write each value to LED pins
    analogWrite(9, map(analogRead(A0),0,1023,0,255));
    analogWrite(10, map(analogRead(A1),0,1023,0,255));
    analogWrite(11, map(analogRead(A2),0,1023,0,255));
}
```

Lesson 8

Activity 1 – Finding Light Levels

```
void setup() {
    Serial.begin(9600); //begin serial monitor at 9600 baud rate
}

void loop() {
    Serial.println(analogRead(A0)); //print analog pin value to
            //serial monitor
    delay(500); //delay 500 ms (makes it easier to read serial
            //monitor values)
}
```

Activity 2 – Using Light Levels

```
int photo = A0; //photoresistor pin
int LED = 9; //LED pin
int sevSeg[] = {2,3,4,5,6,7,8}; //seven segment display pins

// Seven-segment pin layout:
//      4
// 3        5
//      2
// 6        8
//      7

// arrays for displaying each number
// Pins:        2,3,4,5,6,7,8
int one[]   = {0,0,0,1,0,0,1};
int two[]   = {1,0,1,1,1,1,0};
int three[] = {1,0,1,1,0,1,1};
int four[]  = {1,1,0,1,0,0,1};
int five[]  = {1,1,1,0,0,1,1};
int six[]   = {1,1,1,0,1,1,1};

void setup() {
    //for loop to set seven segment pins to output
    for(int i = 2; i < 9; i++){
```

```arduino
      pinMode(i, OUTPUT);
    }
    pinMode(LED, OUTPUT); //set LED pin to output
}

void loop() {
  int prVal = analogRead(photo); //read photoresistor value

  //each part of the if/else if statement writes a pre-
  //calculated value to the LED and has a for loop that sets each
  //LED to 0/1 based on corresponding die value array change
  //comparison values to represent readings from assignment 1

  if(prVal > 780){ //Seven segment value: 6
    analogWrite(LED, 255);
    for(int i = 0; i < 7; i++){
      digitalWrite(sevSeg[i],six[i]);
    }
  }
  else if(prVal > 630){ //Seven segment value: 5
    analogWrite(LED, 213);
    for(int i = 0; i < 7; i++){
      digitalWrite(sevSeg[i],five[i]);
    }
  }
  else if(prVal > 480){ //Seven segment value: 4
    analogWrite(LED, 171);
    for(int i = 0; i < 7; i++){
      digitalWrite(sevSeg[i],four[i]);
    }
  }
  else if(prVal > 330){ //Seven segment value: 3
    analogWrite(LED, 129);
    for(int i = 0; i < 7; i++){
      digitalWrite(sevSeg[i],three[i]);
    }
  }
  else if(prVal > 180){ //Seven segment value: 2
    analogWrite(LED, 87);
    for(int i = 0; i < 7; i++){
      digitalWrite(sevSeg[i],two[i]);
    }
  }
  else if (prVal > 30){ //Seven segment value: 1
    analogWrite(LED, 45);
    for(int i = 0; i < 7; i++){
      digitalWrite(sevSeg[i],one[i]);
    }
  }
  else{ //Turn LED and seven segment display off
    analogWrite(LED, 0);
    for(int i = 0; i < 7; i++){
```

```
        digitalWrite(sevSeg[i],LOW);
      }
    }
}
```

Lesson 9

Activity 1 – Ultrasonic Alarm

```
int trigPin = 9; //ultrasonic trig pin
int echoPin = 10; //ultrasonic echo pin

//LED pins
int green = 4;
int yellow = 5;
int red = 6;

int buzzer = 7; //buzzer pin

void setup() {
  //set ultrasonic pins
  pinMode(trigPin, OUTPUT);
  pinMode(echoPin, INPUT);

  //set LED pins to output
  pinMode(green, OUTPUT);
  pinMode(yellow, OUTPUT);
  pinMode(red, OUTPUT);

  //set buzzer pins to output
  pinMode(buzzer, OUTPUT);

  //turn LEDs off
  digitalWrite(green, LOW);
  digitalWrite(yellow, LOW);
  digitalWrite(red, LOW);
}

void loop() {

  digitalWrite(trigPin, LOW); //send low signal from trig pin to
          //make sure pin is cleared
  delayMicroseconds(2); //delay 2 ms to ensure low signal
          //registers in echo pin

  digitalWrite(trigPin, HIGH); //set trig pin to high to send
          //ping
  delayMicroseconds(10); //delay 10 ms for ping to send
  digitalWrite(trigPin, LOW); //set trig pin to low to end ping

  //pulseIn function will measure the duration of time to receive
  //ping on echo pin
```

```
    long duration = pulseIn(echoPin, HIGH);

    int distance = duration * 0.0343 / 2; //calculate distance
            //using speed of sound

    if(distance <= 15){ //if 15 cm or less
      //turn on red light (green and yellow turn off)
      digitalWrite(green, LOW);
      digitalWrite(yellow, LOW);
      digitalWrite(red, HIGH);

      tone(buzzer, 300); //play tone on buzzer to indicate close
            //proximity
    }
    else if(distance > 15 and distance <= 30){ //if distance 16-30
            //cm
      //turn on yellow light (green and red turn off)
      digitalWrite(green, LOW);
      digitalWrite(yellow, HIGH);
      digitalWrite(red, LOW);

      noTone(buzzer); //ensure buzzer is off
    }
    else{
      //turn on green light (yellow and red turn off)
      digitalWrite(green, HIGH);
      digitalWrite(yellow, LOW);
      digitalWrite(red, LOW);

      noTone(buzzer); //ensure buzzer is off
    }
}
```

Lesson 10

Activity 1 – Hello World

```
#include <LiquidCrystal_I2C.h>

LiquidCrystal_I2C lcd(0x27, 16, 2); //create LCD object

void setup(){
  lcd.init(); //initialize the lcd
  lcd.backlight(); //turn on the backlight
  delay(2000); //delay 2 seconds to make sure display is
            //initialized

  lcd.setCursor(0, 0); //set cursor to row 0, column 0
  lcd.print("Hello World"); // display Hello World on display
}

void loop(){ }
```

Activity 2 – Stopwatch

```cpp
#include <LiquidCrystal_I2C.h>

//button pins
int ssButton = 2;
int resetButton = 3;

//integers to hold pin readings
int ssButtonVal;
long startVal;

//flags to indicate if stopwatch has been started/stopped or
//reset
bool running = false;
bool reset = true;

LiquidCrystal_I2C lcd(0x27, 16, 2); //create new LCD object

void setup()
{
  //set button pins to input
  pinMode(ssButton, INPUT);
  pinMode(resetButton, INPUT);

  lcd.init(); //initialize the lcd
  lcd.backlight(); //turn on the backlight

  //display blank time on the top row
  lcd.setCursor(0, 0);
  lcd.print("Time: 00:00.000");

  //display button titles on the bottom row
  lcd.setCursor(0, 1);
  lcd.print("Start/Stop Reset");
}

void loop()
{
  ssButtonVal = digitalRead(ssButton); //read value of start/stop
          //button

  //if start/stop button is pressed and stopwatch is not yet
  //running, start the stopwatch
  while(ssButtonVal == HIGH and running == false){
    ssButtonVal = digitalRead(ssButton); //read value of
          //start/stop button
    startVal = millis(); //get current runtime of program

    //calculate timer time from previous runtime and current
    //runtime (if timer has been stopped and restarted)
    if(reset == false){startVal = millis()-currVal;}
```

```
    while(ssButtonVal == LOW){ //make sure button press is
            //finished
      reset = false; //set reset flag to false (time is no longer
            //0 and thus not reset)
      running = true; //set running flag to true (stopwatch is
            //now running)

      int currVal = millis() - startVal; // calculate the current
            //time value by finding current millis and subtracting
            //the start time
      int minutes = currVal / 60000; // calculate minutes
            //(integer) by dividing the current time value by
            //60000
      int seconds = (currVal % 60000)/ 1000; // calculate seconds
            //(integer) by dividing the current value by 1000
      int millisecs = currVal % 1000; // calculate milliseconds
            //by finding the remainder of dividing the current
            //time value by 1000 (modulus)

      //the sprintf function formats data to be displayed on the
      //lcd the string of characters gets saved to the char array
      //timeDisp
      char timeDisp[9];
      sprintf(timeDisp, "%02d:%02d.%03d", minutes, seconds,
                millisecs);

      lcd.setCursor(6, 0); //set lcd cursor to column 6, row 0
      lcd.print(timeDisp); //print timeDisp array to lcd

      ssButtonVal = digitalRead(ssButton); //read value of
            //start/stop button
    }
}

//if start/stop button is pressed and stopwatch is already
//running, stop the stopwatch
while(ssButtonVal == HIGH and running == true){
    ssButtonVal = digitalRead(ssButton); //read value of
            //start/stop button

    while(ssButtonVal == LOW){ //make sure button press is
            //finished
      running = false; //set running flag to false (stopwatch is
            //no longer running)

      //if reset button is pressed and stopwatch has not yet been
      //reset
      if(digitalRead(resetButton) == HIGH and reset == false){
                //reset the time
        reset = true; //set reset flag to true (time has been
                //reset to 0)
```

```
            //display blank time on the top row
            lcd.setCursor(0, 0);
            lcd.print("Time: 00:00.000 ");
        }

        ssButtonVal = digitalRead(ssButton); //read value of
                    //start/stop button
    }
  }
}
```

Lesson 11

Activity 1 – Reading Keys

```
#include <Keypad.h>

int sevSeg[] = {13,12,11,10,A3,A4,A5}; //seven segment display
        //pins

// arrays for displaying each character
int one[]   = {0,0,0,1,0,0,1};
int two[]   = {1,0,1,1,1,1,0};
int three[] = {1,0,1,1,0,1,1};
int four[]  = {1,1,0,1,0,0,1};
int five[]  = {1,1,1,0,0,1,1};
int six[]   = {1,1,1,0,1,1,1};
int seven[] = {0,0,1,1,0,0,1};
int eight[] = {1,1,1,1,1,1,1};
int nine[]  = {1,1,1,1,0,0,1};
int zero[]  = {0,1,1,1,1,1,1};
int a[]     = {1,1,1,1,1,0,1};
int b[]     = {1,1,0,0,1,1,1};
int c[]     = {0,1,1,0,1,1,0};
int d[]     = {1,0,0,1,1,1,1};
int pound[] = //fill in your own display
int ast[]   = //fill in your own display

const byte ROWS = 4; //keypad has four rows
const byte COLS = 4; //keypad has four columns
char keys[ROWS][COLS] = { //array for keypad character layout
  {'1','2','3','A'},
  {'4','5','6','B'},
  {'7','8','9','C'},
  {'#','0','*','D'}
};

byte rowPins[ROWS] = {9,8,7,6}; //connect to the row pinouts of
        //the keypad
byte colPins[COLS] = {5,4,3,2}; //connect to the column pinouts
        //of the keypad
```

```
//create new keypad object
Keypad keypad = Keypad( makeKeymap(keys), rowPins, colPins, ROWS,
COLS );

void setup(){
  //for loop to set seven segment pins to output
  for(int i=0; i < 8; i++){
    pinMode(sevSeg[i],OUTPUT);
  }
}

void loop(){
  char key = keypad.getKey(); //get current pressed key

  if (key != NO_KEY){ //if a key is pressed
    switch(key){ //switch statement contains cases for each
         //possible keypad value
      //each case has a for loop that sets each segment to 0/1
      //based on corresponding character value array
      case '1':
        for(int i = 0; i < 8; i++){
          digitalWrite(sevSeg[i],one[i]);
        }
        break;
      case '2':
        for(int i = 0; i < 8; i++){
          digitalWrite(sevSeg[i],two[i]);
        }
        break;
      case '3':
        for(int i = 0; i < 8; i++){
          digitalWrite(sevSeg[i],three[i]);
        }
        break;
      case '4':
        for(int i = 0; i < 8; i++){
          digitalWrite(sevSeg[i],four[i]);
        }
        break;
      case '5':
        for(int i = 0; i < 8; i++){
          digitalWrite(sevSeg[i],five[i]);
        }
        break;
      case '6':
        for(int i = 0; i < 8; i++){
          digitalWrite(sevSeg[i],six[i]);
        }
        break;
      case '7':
        for(int i = 0; i < 8; i++){
```

```arduino
        digitalWrite(sevSeg[i],seven[i]);
      }
      break;
   case '8':
      for(int i = 0; i < 8; i++){
        digitalWrite(sevSeg[i],eight[i]);
      }
      break;
   case '9':
      for(int i = 0; i < 8; i++){
        digitalWrite(sevSeg[i],nine[i]);
      }
      break;
   case '0':
      for(int i = 0; i < 8; i++){
        digitalWrite(sevSeg[i],zero[i]);
      }
      break;
   case 'A':
      for(int i = 0; i < 8; i++){
        digitalWrite(sevSeg[i],a[i]);
      }
      break;
   case 'B':
      for(int i = 0; i < 8; i++){
        digitalWrite(sevSeg[i],b[i]);
      }
      break;
   case 'C':
      for(int i = 0; i < 8; i++){
        digitalWrite(sevSeg[i],c[i]);
      }
      break;
   case 'D':
      for(int i = 0; i < 8; i++){
        digitalWrite(sevSeg[i],d[i]);
      }
      break;
   case '#':
      for(int i = 0; i < 8; i++){
        digitalWrite(sevSeg[i],pound[i]);
      }
      break;
   case '*':
      for(int i = 0; i < 8; i++){
        digitalWrite(sevSeg[i],ast[i]);
      }
      break;
    }
  }
}
```

Lesson 12

Activity 1 – Scoreboard

```cpp
#include <Keypad.h>
#include <LiquidCrystal_I2C.h>

// To use scoreboard:
// - Press button A/B to choose home/away
// - Press number keys to enter score
// - Press # to set score after entering
// - Press * to reset score to 0

int colPos = 0; //column position variable will be updated based on
          //home/away selection

LiquidCrystal_I2C lcd(0x27, 16, 2); //create new LCD object

const byte ROWS = 4; //keypad has four rows
const byte COLS = 4; //keypad has four columns
char keys[ROWS][COLS] = { //array for keypad character layout
  {'1','2','3','A'},
  {'4','5','6','B'},
  {'7','8','9','C'},
  {'*','0','#','D'}
};
byte rowPins[ROWS] = {9,8,7,6}; //connect to the row pinouts of the
          //keypad
byte colPins[COLS] = {5,4,3,2}; //connect to the column pinouts of the
          //keypad

Keypad keypad = Keypad( makeKeymap(keys), rowPins, colPins, ROWS, COLS
          ); //create new keypad object

void setup() {
  lcd.init(); //initialize the lcd
  lcd.backlight(); //turn on the backlight

  //display heading on top row
  lcd.setCursor(0, 0);
  lcd.print("  Home    Away");
}

void loop() {
  char teamKey = keypad.getKey(); //get key press for home/away
          //selection

  if (teamKey != NO_KEY){ //if key is pressed

    //set column position based on home/away selection
    if(teamKey == 'A'){ colPos = 2; }
    else if(teamKey == 'B'){ colPos = 10; }
```

```
    char scoreKey = keypad.getKey(); //get key press for score input

  if(colPos != 0){ //if colPos is not 0, then a team has been
          //selected
    lcd.setCursor(colPos, 1); //set cursor to colPos on row 1
    lcd.print("        "); //clear score by writing over current
          //score with spaces
    lcd.setCursor(colPos, 1); //set cursor to colPos on row 1
    lcd.blink(); //blink cursor so user knows program is ready to
          //have score entered

    while(scoreKey != '#'){ //while score is being entered
      //if key pressed is a number or *
      if(scoreKey != NO_KEY and scoreKey != 'A' and scoreKey != 'B'
                  and scoreKey != 'C' and scoreKey != 'D'){
        if(scoreKey == '*'){ //if * pressed then reset score to 0
              //for selected team
          lcd.setCursor(colPos, 1); //set cursor to colPos on row 1
          lcd.print("        "); //print over score with spaces
          lcd.setCursor(colPos, 1); //set cursor to colPos on row 1
          lcd.print('0'); //print 0 as new score
          break; //exit while loop
        }

        lcd.print(scoreKey); //print pressed number to screen
      }
      scoreKey = keypad.getKey(); //get next key press
    }
  }

  lcd.noBlink(); //stop blinking cursor since score entering is
          //finished
  colPos = 0; //reset column position to 0
  }
}
```

Lesson 13

Activity 1 – Changing Speeds (Version 1)

```
    int motorPin = 9; //set pin number for motor control pin
    int potPin = A0; //set pin number for potentiometr

    void setup() {
      pinMode(motorPin, OUTPUT); //set motor control pin to output
    }

    void loop() {
      //read the potentiometer pin and map the value from the analog
      //range 0-1023 to the pwm range 0-255
      int pwmVal = map(analogRead(potPin),0,1023,0,255);
```

```
    //write the mapped value to the motor control pin
    analogWrite(motorPin,pwmVal);
}
```

Activity 1 – Changing Speeds (Version 2)

```
void setup() {
    pinMode(9, OUTPUT); //set motor control pin to output
}

void loop() {
    //read the potentiometer pin and map the value from the analog
    //range 0-1023 to the pwm range 0-255
    //and write the mapped value to the motor control pin
    analogWrite(9,map(analogRead(A0),0,1023,0,255));
}
```

Lesson 14

Activity 1 – Point the Way

```
#include <Servo.h>

Servo myServo; //create new servo object
int servoPos = 0; //integer to hold servo position

void setup() {
    //attach servo to pin 9 and write current servoPos (0)
    myServo.attach(9);
    myServo.write(servoPos);

    //set button pins to input
    pinMode(2,INPUT);
    pinMode(3, INPUT);
}

void loop() {
    //while button 1 is pressed and servo is not at minimum value
    while(digitalRead(2) == HIGH and servoPos > 0){
        servoPos--; //decrement servo position integer
        myServo.write(servoPos); //write new position value
        delay(5); //delay 5 milliseconds to allow for servo movement
    }

    //while button 2 is pressed and servo is not at maximum value
    while(digitalRead(3) == HIGH and servoPos < 180){
        servoPos++; //increment servo position integer
        myServo.write(servoPos); //write new position value
        delay(5); //delay 5 milliseconds to allow for servo movement
    }
}
```

Activity 2 – Garage Door Opener

```cpp
#include <Servo.h>

Servo myServo; //create new servo object

int posFlag = 0; //position flag (0 - closed, 1 - open)
int newFlag = 1; //button press flag (1 indicates new button
          //press)

void setup() {
  //attach servo to pin 9 and write value of 0
  myServo.attach(9);
  myServo.write(0);

  pinMode(2,INPUT); //set button pin to input
}

void loop() {
  newFlag = 1; //set new button press flag to 1 as button press
          //has not occurred
  int buttonVal = digitalRead(2); //read button pin

  while(buttonVal == HIGH){ //while button is pressed
    //if current servo position is 180 and button press is new
    if(posFlag == 1 and newFlag == 1){
      //set servo position to 0 - a for loop decrementing 180-0
      //with delay function is used to achieve smooth movement
      //through the range of values

      for(int i = 180; i >= 0; i--){
        myServo.write(i);
        delay(5);
      }

      posFlag = 0; //set position flag to 0 (new servo position
              //0)
      newFlag = 0; //set new button press to 0 (button press has
              //been fulfilled)
    }

    if(posFlag == 0 and newFlag == 1){
      //set servo position to 180 - a for loop incrementing 0-180
      //with delay function is used to achieve smooth movement
      //through the range of values

      for(int i = 0; i <= 180; i++){
        myServo.write(i);
        delay(5);
      }
      posFlag = 1; //set position flag to 1 (new servo position
              //180)
      newFlag = 0; //set new button press to 0 (button press has
```

```
                          //been fulfilled)
        }

      buttonVal = digitalRead(2); //read button pin
    }
  }
```

Lesson 15
Activity 1 – Temperature Controlled Fan

```cpp
#include <Servo.h>

Servo myServo; //create new servo object

void setup() {
  myServo.attach(10); //attach servo to pin 10
  pinMode(6, OUTPUT); //set DC motor control pin to output
}

void loop() {
  int sensorVal = analogRead(A0); //read temperature sensor pin

  //equations to convert analog value into voltage and
  //temperature values
  float voltage = sensorVal * (5.0 / 1024.0);
  float tempC = (voltage - 0.5) * 100;
  float tempF = (tempC * 9.0 / 5.0) + 32.0;

  //for each temperature range, write a pwm value to the DC motor
  //control pin and set servo motor to given position
  if(tempF > 100){
    analogWrite(6,80);
    myServo.write(144);
  }
  else if(tempF > 77){
    analogWrite(6,70);
    myServo.write(108);
  }
  else if(tempF > 50){
    analogWrite(6,60);
    myServo.write(72);
  }
  else{
    analogWrite(6,0);
    myServo.write(36);
  }

  delay(3000);
}
```

Lesson 16

Activity 1 – Stepper Motor Timer

```cpp
#include <Stepper.h>

//set LED pin values
int red = 3;
int green = 5;
int blue = 6;

//set buzzer and button pin values
int piezo = 7;
int button = 12;

Stepper myStepper(2048, 8, 10, 9, 11);

void setup() {
  //set LED pins to output
  pinMode(red,OUTPUT);
  pinMode(green,OUTPUT);
  pinMode(blue,OUTPUT);

  //blue light on to indicate timer is not running
  digitalWrite(green, LOW);
  digitalWrite(red, LOW);
  digitalWrite(blue, HIGH);

  //initialize buzzer and button pins
  pinMode(piezo,OUTPUT);
  pinMode(button,INPUT);
}

void loop() {
  if(digitalRead(button) == HIGH){ //if button pressed - start
        //timer
    //turn blue light off and green light on
    digitalWrite(blue, LOW);
    digitalWrite(green, HIGH);

    //move stepper for 45 seconds (1536 steps at 1 rpm)
    myStepper.setSpeed(1);
    myStepper.step(1536);

    digitalWrite(red, HIGH); //turn red light on (green + red =
        //yellow)
    myStepper.step(341); //move stepper for 10 seconds

    digitalWrite(green, LOW); //turn green light off (red stays
        //on)
    myStepper.step(171); //move stepper for 5 seconds
```

```
    digitalWrite(red, LOW); //turn red light off

    //play tone on buzzer for 3 seconds, then turn off
    tone(piezo, 440);
    delay(3000);
    noTone(piezo);

  }
  digitalWrite(blue, HIGH); //turn blue light back on to indicate
          //timer is finished
}
```

www.ingramcontent.com/pod-product-compliance
Lightning Source LLC
LaVergne TN
LVHW081756050326
832903LV00027B/1974